Young Men

And

Fast Machines

A Story of Muscle Cars in the Sixties

William A. Bowers, Jr.

ISBN: 979-8-9918539-1-0
Library of Congress Control Number:
2025916429
Published by

Swampfox Publishing Company

Edited by Deloris W. Bowers and Liz B. Hall
Interior Design by William A. Bowers, III
Cover Design by William A. Bowers, Jr.

Printed in the USA for Swampfox Publishing Company

YOUNG MEN AND FAST MACHINES

Table of Contents

Picture Index

Forward

I know beyond a shadow of a doubt that had I lived 125 years ago, I would've been one of those with a fast horse. When I was young, I used to like to ride my bicycle fast with the wind blowing in my face. I only had a one speed bike but I had dreamed of having an English racer so I could go faster.

As I got older one of my friends had horses. I would get out of school in the seventh grade, hustle to the house, jump on my bike and race cross-country through the woods to his house. I would almost always beat his bus to his house and would be waiting as he climbed off the bus. His father had set down the law. If we wanted to ride horses we would have to feed the hogs first. We would jump on the little Farmall tractors and to the trailer and run the quarter-mile down to the hog pens to feed up. Afterward we would go catch up and saddle the quarter horses. We would ride in the fields and in the woods until it was time for me to head home and for me to be there before dark. I looked forward to that and of the fun we had racing those quarter horses. My friend got a big paint, named King, who was without a doubt the fastest horse in the county. We would race him against people's cars on the dirt road to the point where when the car came by, he thought he was supposed to race. The horse I liked to ride was a black Marsh Pony off Cumberland Island. Since he was born wild, he was the fastest in the woods.

As I grew older and got my first car, although it was not fast, I drove it as fast as I could. I fell in love with quarter-mile drag racing. There is something about revving the engine up, releasing the clutch and accelerating for all the car was worth. It was fun even in cars that were not fast but became much more fun with the faster cars. There was something about hearing a big V-8 with straight exhaust rev up and then when the clutch was dumped hearing the tires squall and hear that big V-8 as the RPM's increased. Some of them sounded as if they almost were going to blow up when the driver would catch another gear and start the sequence all over again. I can remember going to the drag strip and watching some remarkable gassers and rail dragsters and later funny cars as they ran down the track. We even had a jet dragster one time that was extremely fast. I don't remember what elapsed time it ran I just remember how loud it was and how hard the exhaust would blow on you as he went by.

In elementary school, I was a fan of the Ferraris since they were born the same year as me. I always wanted one but to this day have yet to afford such a fancy ride. I fell in love with road races and endurance races. I love to hear them gear down as they went into the turns of them run back up through the gears. I can hear the tires protesting as they made the way into a turn and the car pushed on the tires almost breaking loose into a spin. To this day I would've liked to have run in the 24 hours at Daytona or the 12 hours at Sebring or even better the 24 hours at Le Mans.

NASCAR became something that I was very interested in. For several years I would not miss 4th of July race at Daytona International Speedway. We would go there at night because at midnight the Paul Revere 250 would begin. Mustangs, Cougars, Camaros, Firebirds and all forms of sport cars from the fastest to the slower small cars down to the Mini Cooper that reminded me of a matchbox with four little wheels on it. They would race for 250 miles incorporating the trioval part of the Speedway with the flat inside portion of the track for a distance of 3.9 miles per lap. I remember sitting in the infield with my buddies, sharing stories of our favorite cars and drivers. We got to see some of the best road racers that also raced the NASCAR circuit because they would race that night in the 250 and then before noon the next day would crank up the big block V-8 Detroit cars to run the trioval.

I also remember going to dirt track races here in my hometown. Some of the Good Old Boys that later became famous on the NASCAR circuit raced right out here at Dunn's Lake.

After I was out of school and had become part of the working class, I was able to put the money I made to get my faster cars and of course later my fastest car. I still cannot go to the races without getting excited. I can smell the rubber burning and it sets off some genes deep inside my body, the genes that like to go fast.

Some folks even used to race boats in the Altamaha River and in other places. We had folks around here with a reputation of really being able to build a fast boat and tune a fast motor. I can still hear him coming down the Altamaha River with those engines screaming as they turned up the RPM's. My father told me of when Sir Malcolm Campbell had the Bluebird on Daytona Beach when he was a young man. He and his brother used to race Model A's on the beach course there at Daytona. I guess I must've inherited the "Need for Speed".

In this compilation of stories, you will quickly find that I was not the only one in my age group that loved to drive fast. Maybe I can give you a little insight on what it was like to be a young man during the "Age of the Muscle Car". And to let you know how we all managed to stay alive and out of jail even though we did love to run fast.

The Beginning of an Era

Although it began in the 1950's, the era of fast cars began to bloom in the 1960's. There came a time when almost everyone had a fast car and muscle cars were a dime a dozen. Bear with me as I reflect upon those times and am brought into remembrance of the days of yesteryear. This is an effort to ensure that all the old stories we have shared about those "Muscle Car Days" do not die but remain with us in perpetuity. This was the most exciting time of my life where I took chances that I most likely should not have but due to the "Need for Speed" that was deeply embedded in me, I involved myself up to the hilt in it.

I once told someone that had I been born 100 years earlier there is no doubt that I would have owned one of the fastest horses around, if possible. I most likely would have loved the feel of the wind blowing in my face as I sped along on my trusty steed. Matter of fact, when I was young, I did like to ride horses. I did like to ride them fast. So, there is no doubt that what I speak of would have been certain.

The invention that probably saved me as an older adult was cruise control. If I depended upon my foot, I most likely would still be speeding down the countryside. I would probably have a collection of speeding tickets from everywhere I traveled. Fortunately, I have only collected two speeding tickets in my life. I now set the cruise control even on really short trips. This has saved me a lot of money in fines, and much embarrassment from having been seen pulled off on the side of the road with those blue lights flashing.

Naturally, when I became old enough to own automobiles, I still wanted to go fast. Unfortunately for me, my first vehicle was a 1947 Chevrolet that I never got to drive but about twice before it was relegated to the junkyard. You see, my grandfather had given that to me, and it broke my heart when the junkman came and hauled it off that day. The first automobile that I bought was a 1955 four-door Chevrolet from my parents. It had a whopping 235 cubic inch six-cylinder engine. It came equipped with a power glide two speed automatic transmission. It was not fast, but it was a way of getting from point A to point B. I drove it until the Powerglide failed, due to the fact that the repair of the transmission cost more than the car was worth, it also made a trip to the junkyard. Needless to say, I didn't have anything fast enough for me to be drag racing with at the time. When I bought my little Falcon, which was not fast, but had a standard transmission so you could "Squeal A Wheel", I did in fact enter it into some drag races both on the track and on the highway. Winning some and losing some. My next vehicle, which was my 1966 fastback Mustang, was fast for its class. You see a fastback weighed about 300 pounds more than a coupe and therefore was placed one class lower due to the horsepower to weight ratio. I won lots of trophies with that Mustang. I raced many grudge races at the drag strip with it. This is where I found that since I only had the one shift to make, due to an extremely high geared rear axle (2.80 to 1), that I could in fact beat the lighter Mustang coupes.

First Drag Racing Trophy

Bowers Collection

1964 Fairlane Station Wagon

My First Cars

When I turned 16, my family purchased a brand-new 1964 Ford Fairlane station wagon. This was equipped with a 260 cubic inch, 2-barrel carbureted engine. I had saved up money from my job and purchased their 1955 Chevrolet four door sedan. Being a four-door it was not as snazzy as a two-door version, but it did provide transportation and got me back and forth to where I wanted to go. Fast, it was not, but it did look pretty good to me as it was white over turquoise. I drove it until the transmission broke and ended up selling it for junk too.

I actually had a poor start with automobile ownership. Although I had been studying Ferrari for years (since Ferrari was born in 1947 the same year as me) I soon realized that I would probably never make enough money to own one. When I was about 13 years old, I was riding my bicycle to the movie when I spotted a car over by the Sheriff's office. I immediately recognized it as a Ferrari. I pulled over to it with my bicycle and got off to look. I was looking all over the car, just amazed, trying to figure out what a Ferrari was doing in Baxley, Georgia. The sheriff emerged from his office and scolded me, wanting to know what I was doing. I told him I was looking at this Ferrari.

"This what?" He asked with a puzzled look on his face.

"This is a 1958 Ferrari 250 Gran Turismo!" I replied excitedly "You know that it has a V-12 engine with six Weber two-barrel side throat carburetors on it, don't you?"

1958 Ferrari 250 Gran Turismo

He had a strange look on his face. I later discovered they had found the Ferrari in a cornfield out in the county and found out it had been stolen in Atlanta, Georgia. The sheriff had almost scared the deputy to death on the way back to town driving it, because the sheriff liked fast cars too. A good example of how he liked fast cars is that one of his sheriff cars was a 1963 ½ Ford Galaxy 500 XL with a 406 cubic inch engine, with three two-barrel carburetors sitting atop it with a four-speed top loader transmission in it. The car was jet black with gold lettering indicating it was the Appling County Sheriff.

The 1950's, the Beginnings of Fast Cars

In the early fifties there were not many fast cars. Fords had a flathead small cubic inch V8. Most others had either straight six-cylinder engines with some straight eight-cylinder engines. The change began when the Corvettes emerged on the scene. They were soon followed by the Thunderbirds, Mercurys and the Crown Victoria Fords with small cubic inch V-8 engines in the police interceptor variation. All manufacturers had a police interceptor engine which generally meant it had a four-barrel carburetor instead of a two-barrel. They were in fact faster than the standard equipped engine. In 1955 Chevrolet had a 265 cubic inch Powerpack engine and Super Powerpack. A friend of mine had a sister whose boyfriend had a Corvette, but most everybody else had automobiles with little, slow, small cubic inch engines. Ford had the 272 cubic inch and then the 292 cubic inch in their police interceptor models. I can remember one friend of mine had a 1952 Pontiac with a straight eight in it. By 1955 or 1956 most top engines were V8's and had started to become larger in cubic inch displacement.

My friend Darrell's future brother-in-law had a 1954 Corvette (this was before they became "Stingrays"). I thought that it was about as awesome a car as I had ever seen at the time. Although it sported Chevrolet's 235 cubic inch inline six-cylinder engine, the "Cool Factor" was high for that offering.

I do remember the 1955, 1956 and 1957 Thunderbirds. They were also "Super Cool". In 1958 they changed and were less desirable to me, although at one time I entertained purchasing a dolled up one when I was in the market for a snazzy ride.

1957 was a banner year with all the manufacturers having fast cars. Ford had just introduced the new 312 cubic inch that even came in a supercharged version in the Thunderbird. Chevrolet had the 283 cubic inch fuel injection V-8. Dodge and Plymouth had their 318. Two brothers that were friends of mine, Jimmy and Robert, had a 1957 Pontiac Bonneville Special, with a 347 cubic inch fuel injected V-8 that was really fast for that time. Two of my friends from Virginia owned one of these.

By 1958 engine sizes were again increased. Chevrolet had a 348 cubic inch and due to Ford introducing the Edsel and also introduced what was to be termed the FE Block. This was a 332 cubic inch then later a 352 cubic inch FE engine. All the other manufacturers had the fast police interceptor, even the Studebaker had their Golden Hawk version which was very fast. All the hot engines produced around 300 horsepower, which was a load of horsepower for that day and time.

In the early 1960's engines got bigger and better. Chevrolet had its 348 cubic inch which morphed into the 409 cubic inch. Ford had the 352 then the 390 cubic inch and later the 406 cubic inch engines as options. Dodge and Plymouth had the 383 cubic inch followed by the 413 cubic inch. They came in all variations of dispensing fuel into the engine. There were four barrels, three deuces, fuel injection and blown engines.

By the mid 1960's to the late 1960's engine sizes had grown, Chevrolet had its 427 cubic inch. Ford had its 427 cubic inch and 428 cubic inch. Chrysler Corporation had the 426 cubic inch hemispherical head (Hemi) and the 440 cubic inch either with a 4-barrel carburetor or the "Six Pack", equipped with three two-barrel carburetors. Oldsmobile had jumped into the mix along with Pontiac and Buick. Mercury had joined Ford with its fast cars.

7

There were even cars like the Avanti from Studebaker which had advanced in leaps and bounds.

The first guys to have cars with the big engines, (which were generally in family cars to start with), were the ones whose family had unknowingly bought the cars with those large engines in them. I had two friends who drove their parent's family car, a 409 cubic inch Chevrolet Impala. In 1965 a friend of mine bought someone's former family car which was a 1961 Ford Starliner with a 352 cubic inch police interceptor in it. Most of us were so poor we were behind the curve and had to settle for much less than that.

My 1955 Chevy

Bowers Collection

When I acquired our family car which was a 1955 Chevrolet four-door Bel Air. The color was white over aquamarine. This was a beautiful color scheme if only it had been a two-door instead of a four-door. The vehicle was not what you would consider fast. At that time my parents had bought a Fairlane 500 station wagon which came equipped with a 260 cubic inch 2-barrel carbureted engine and a two speed Ford automatic transmission.

While I was in high school my friend, Roy, had a 1952 Pontiac with a "straight eight". It was a whopping 268 cubic inch power plant. He would pick me up for school in it. It had a weird speedometer. When he would accelerate, the speedometer would register 120 miles per hour within a city block. The car was not that fast, but the speedometer surely was.

When my 1955 was running I would follow two of my friends before school. They would race through a developing subdivision that still had dirt streets. One guy, Buddy, had a baby blue 1958 Chevy and the other, Darrell, had a black and white 1958 Chevy. They were both faster than my 1955. They would sometimes "clean out the ditches" in that subdivision which would disturb the residents.

One morning after the bell rang, the sheriff came to the school parking lot with Buddy's hubcap in his hand. It did not take long for him to identify Buddy as one of the culprits. He did not rat anyone else out and took all the blame. Afterward we slowed down terrorizing that neighborhood. Both Darrell and Buddy are no longer with us as I write this.

My 1955 Chevy lasted until one of my friends, who was driving, revved it up to a high RPM in neutral and snatched it into low gear, which destroyed the powerglide automatic transmission. Upon getting estimates on the cost of rebuilding that powerglide, we made the decision that it was time to junk the old 1955 Chevy. This move put me afoot again and relegated me to either hitching rides or borrowing the family Fairlane for dates. This was not a good situation for a teenage boy in South Georgia or anywhere else.

1955 Ford Convertible

Bowers Collection

My friends Lamar, Ray and I used to hang out together. I had to wait until I was 16 to get my 1955 Chevrolet, but at 15 years old, Ray had somehow managed to buy a 1955 Ford convertible from a sailor at Glynco Naval Air Base in Brunswick, Georgia. Ray was about a month older than me and was absolutely not 16 when he got that thing. It was painted "Navy Blue" and I believe that that sailor painted it with U.S. Navy paint intended for airplanes. It was a good-looking car, and the girls seemed to like it quite a lot. I don't even remember what engine was in it, but I do remember two distinct things about it. The first was that the radio had a part called a vibrator that would constantly die. Ray was forced to keep a good stock of them in the car to keep the radio working, which was essential when dating. The second was that for some reason unknown to us, if it choked down, it was hard to crank the doggone thing. We learned to park it on a grade where we could get it rolling in order to pop the clutch and crank it. Although there was one day when I pushed it all over the flat landscape of Jekyll Island trying to get it to crank. If you were planning to make a fast getaway, with that flat topography, you better not shut the doggone thing off.

One night Ray, Luther and I were triple dating in that car. We got out on a sandy dirt road just out of Baxley, when the girl Ray was with, Judy, wanted to drive. I told him he better not let her drive because this would be an awful place to try to push the car off in those sand beds. Her brother was a renowned hot rodder around town, and she professed that she could drive just as good as him. Ray relented and let her under the wheel. When she let the clutch out, the car choked down in the middle of the sand bed on that dirt road. We were in a bind. In a little while we saw car lights coming our way. It was a group of men that lived in that neighborhood, which was kind of on the rough side. They agreed to help us push the car. As it turned out, I was the only one of the occupants they got out to push it. Ray was under the wheel and Luther had stayed in the car. There I was at the back bumper with all of those unsavory characters, pushing when the little dark blue Ford fired off. To this day, I don't know if Ray intended to leave me or did not realize I was still back there, but he gunned it with all of those guys hollering for him to stop. I guess he didn't know what they wanted and thought that I was in the car, which I was not. I am really not sure how I got back into the car, other than I was holding on to the convertible top and somehow straightened my legs, like unto Roy Rogers, and bounced over into the back seat. To this day I do not know how I did that, but I did not think I wanted to be left with that group of unsavory characters because I knew there was no way I could hold my own in a fight with that many. When we finally got back into town, I told Ray to never let that girl drive again. I don't care if her brother is the best driver in town or a NASCAR champion, she's not driving with me in there.

I used to go to Brunswick to visit Ray and to hang out with him on a regular basis. Even when I would go duck hunting at the coast, most times I would stop by and visit before coming back. His family seemed like my second family, at that time.

As a side note Ray and Lamar are no longer with us. They passed within 4 months of each other. It was sad to lose two close friends that close together.

This brings us to the "Muscle Car Era". This was a time when every manufacturer had fast cars, not just one, like in the old police interceptor days but they were all fast up and down the line. There were big cars, medium-size cars, pony cars and even fast compacts. All of them produced lots of horsepower and were very competitive in their day for quarter-mile elapsed time in their class. Although all the manufacturers had their top fast cars, people were quick to choose upsides. They would be in the Bow Time camp, the Mopar camp or the Blue Oval camp for the most part.

1964 Fairlane Station Wagon

During 1965, my friend Jamie and I took my father's 1964 Fairlane station wagon to the drag strip in Vidalia, Georgia. At first, we only went to watch, but then I got a wild hair and decided I would enter the Fairlane and race it. Race it I did. I won a trophy for my efforts. This taste of drag racing became quite expensive to me later on. The thrill of running side by side and beating the car you were racing was exhilarating. I hid the trophy from my mom and dad and although Jamie and I had this picture taken with the car and the trophy I did not mention it for fear I would not get to drive the car anymore.

Although the Fairlane was not very fast I learned to be consistent with my driving. I won a class trophy every time I took it to the dragstrip. Although it would only run about a 16.45 elapsed time, I could replicate that almost every time I ran. There was no trouble with tire spin since the 260 cubic inch powerplant was not beast enough to burn rubber. There was no trouble with missing shifts because all I had to do was move it from low to drive. The thing I learned to do the best was to come off the line with the lights. I have been blessed with super-fast reflexes that I used playing third base in baseball most of my life. Those reflexes translated into being able to react quickly when the light changed. Once at Don Garlis' Museum in Ocala, Florida, my reaction time was measured at .025 seconds which is pretty darn quick.

1960 Falcon

As I was getting prepared to graduate from high school in 1965, I decided to forego the class trip. They would not allow us to go to the Bahamas, and I since had been to New York City the summer before I did not particularly want to go back. I took the money that it would have taken for the class trip and purchased a 1960 Ford Falcon. This was a cute car, black with a white top and was equipped with an 85 horsepower 144 cubic inch in-line six-cylinder and a standard three speed transmission with the shifter on the column. It had white sidewall tires, so I took the cheap hub caps off and painted the rims black. We began to race around the county with other six-cylinder cars. My cousin Lamar and my friend Lewis and some of the local boys would find a desolate piece of road and hold us a "drag race". My little 144 did not make as much horsepower as the 235 Chevrolet's did, although my Falcon was lighter, and the horsepower to weight ratio was not terrible. The three speed standard shift transmission that the Falcon came equipped with was much better for a low horsepower car, if you wanted acceleration. I could run with the Chevrolet's most of the time, and we had some good races.

One night we were racing near one of my cousin's houses, when Lewis and another boy were racing their 235 cubic inch Chevrolet's. At the end of the race for a reason unknown to any of us, the other boy, who was ahead, turned into the lane in front of Lewis, and they had a terrible crash. This tore both cars up badly. This cooled our heels for street racing for a little while.

My father, who was a good mechanic in his own right, had raced along with his brother Gene in the Model A races on Daytona Beach when they were young. He used to kid me about my Falcon. At first, he said that it reminded him so much of the Henry J that he used to own (the one we used to go back-and-forth to Florida and visit relatives) that it was ridiculous. He said all I needed to have to work on that Falcon was a half inch wrench, some bailing wire and some chewing gum. He said those items would repair anything on the little simple car. He taught me quite a bit about mechanic work as he helped me work on it. I was forever tinkering on the darn thing, although I did not know much about working on vehicles. I guess it may have been in my genes. I was forever under the hood and tried to keep the running gear in good shape.

I then began to take my Falcon to the drag strip in Vidalia, Georgia. My elapsed time was somewhere in the neighborhood of 17 seconds, which was a mite slower than the 16 second range that the Fairlane station wagon would run. I honed my ability to be consistent, driving the Falcon. Although I did not have a tachometer, I learned to "Shift by Ear". This consistency carried on in my later vehicles. I did pretty well there for a while, taking a trophy every Sunday. Then a fellow came up with a red Studebaker V8 and although I would jump him off the starting line and would lead him most of the way down the quarter mile, on the far end of the quarter mile stretch that V8 would begin to pull me and although barely, he would outrun me. This got me frustrated and I explored the things that I might be able to do to outperform him in the ¼ mile stretch. I could have outrun him at the Claxton, Georgia Drag strip. Once at the Vidalia, Georgia track, I was revving it real high so as to get a better jump off at the line when one of my buddies said the man on the loudspeaker told the starter "You better let them go, Beach, before that little black one blows up". I don't know how many revolutions per minute I was turning it because I didn't have a tachometer, but I would rev it till it started making really funny sounds. Using my high rev method, my right rear would spin for twenty-seven yards. I could outrun that Studebaker for about 2/3 of the quarter mile before the torque of his V 8 would pull past me. I begged him to come run me the 1/8 mile at the Claxton-Metter Georgia dragstrip, but he would not. After getting tired of being beat by that red "rutabaga" I pulled a stunt on the drag strip officials. I already knew that the straight shift 144's came with solid lifters and also knew there was no difference in the bore of the 144 cubic inch, the 170 cubic inch, and the 200 cubic inch Ford six cylinders, the difference in stroke made the displacement difference. Therefore, when I classified, I told them that my car had solid lifters and the same pistons as 200 cubic inch, which was not a lie. They told me that since I had done all that work to my car, that I could no longer run stock and I would have to run in modified production. To be exact, the class was F Modified Production. I just shrugged my shoulders and said well if that is how it has got to be. Although I still got to run all the cars that I was running, including the red "rutabaga" in grudge races, I had no one else in the class with me so I always brought a trophy home.

I tore the transmission out of that little black Falcon so many times that I could almost rebuild it with my eyes closed. I had stripped the shift tube out to the point that when I was in first gear the shift lever would be pointing directly to the floor and when I was in second gear the lever would point to the ceiling. Finally, I scrapped up enough money to buy an Eelco conversion kit, so I could have the shifter in the floor and not have to mess with the shift tube anymore. I found the Eelco conversion kit that was supposed to fit that Falcon, so I purchased it. I paid a whopping $15 for it. I took it to my garage which was the shade of the giant laurel oak tree in daddy's yard (the same place that I rebuilt that little three speed transmission about seven times) and disconnected all the cutting the hole in the floorboard so as to mount the shifter. Much to my dismay, it did not fit correctly. I had to rig it with two of the transmission shift arms pointing up and two pointing down. This made my shift pattern a little weird. First was to the left and up (like in a four-speed). Second was to the right and up. This left third gear to the right and down. I had taken it out of the box and installed it so I could not return the shifter. That meant I needed to either buy a new shifter (which I did not have money for) or use it as it was. Although the pattern was weird, I learned how to speed shift making the looping motion from first to second. I was the only one that knew how to drive it because no one else could find the correct gear. Since I only had the one shift to make in the quarter mile, I had to make sure that I was really good at it.

19

On one occasion I left college in Douglas, Georgia and had gone looking for a party in Nicholls, Georgia. Upon heading back, I remembered a long hill near the Holiness Baptist Church Campground, so as I approached it, I wound the little Falcon as tight as I could wind it in second gear. I started down the hill with it still in second gear wound tight, and about halfway down the hill I heard the most gosh awful, rattling, clanging sound from my engine compartment. I limped back to Douglas with it only running on three cylinders. The next day I went up to the Texaco station by the college and the mechanic there determined that I had most likely broken a pushrod or two. I went up to Brooks Auto Parts and bought some pushrods. I came back and the guy at the Texaco Station let me use the rear of his station to change the rods, then I proceeded to change them out. I had been careful enough in removing the valve cover that I didn't even have to purchase a new gasket, so I got old Blackie back going again.

We raced those six cylinders up and down the paved country roads around Baxley. We thought we were just the fastest things there could be. I could run with most of the other six cylinders, especially if they would make a mistake shifting or taking off. It's funny now to think about it but back in that day you could buy 13-inch recapped tires to fit the Falcon for just a few dollars. Since the Falcon didn't have a tremendous amount of horsepower, you didn't burn them up much, so you got your money's worth. If I revved that little 85 horsepower six cylinder up, I could spin the right rear tire for the 27 yards as I mentioned. I could swap the tires back and forth on the rear and they would last quite a while. Since the non-pulling wheel never spun, it would remain unhurt. Matter of fact during that time, for economic reasons, I ran recaps all the time on the Falcon and never had any difficulty with them.

A friend of mine, Bruce, whose father had a local filling station, owned a Henry J and George who worked with them, owned a souped-up Rambler with a V8 in it that had been bored and stroked. On Saturday nights we would break out the white shoe polish and write the names of our racecars on the side. My Falcon was named "Mojo" the Henry J was named "Henry VIII" and the Rambler was named "Scrambler". As a side note the filling station was right by the railroad track in the middle of town, and George would park the Rambler in the last parking place parallel to the railroad track, on the street that ran parallel to the track when he was at work. Every once in a while, he would see the Baxley City Police come through and run over there and crank up that Rambler, back in all the way up the street almost a block and then turn it loose. He would burn rubber on those old tires that he had on it to the point that it looked like the mosquito sprayer had come through town. He would never cut his lights on and would always end up in the same place and jump out and run back across the street to the service station. In no time at all, the police would come around, and the smoke would still be drifting in the air, from the tires burning. There the Rambler was still parked in the same place it always was. Bruce and George and I would stand over there and just laugh our heads off. You see we liked to harangue the local police. We weren't mean, we were just mischievous.

1965 Mercury Comet

My cousin, Lamar, got tired of his little yellow six-cylinder Mercury so he acquired a red 289 cubic inch 2-barrel V8 Mercury Comet that was much faster than his little six. I would race him with the Falcon, but there was really no need for he had way too much horsepower for me. (A little later I'll tell a story of what Cousin Lamar did after I got a faster car.)

There was a time when almost everybody was running six-cylinder cars, so cars that had a V8 had so much better horsepower to weight ratio it was awesome. There were a few cars that were reputed to be fast, one friend, Jerry, who was a little older than I, had a Falcon with the 260 Cubic Inch high-performance engine in it. That engine had over 240 horsepower. I never got to see that car run, but I always coveted it. I later found one of them parked in the field in Wheeler County, Georgia but could not locate the owner or I may have purchased it.

1963 Falcon Sprint

One day a fella came to town, working with the telephone company. He had an immaculate 1956 Chevrolet with the 265 cubic inch Powerpack engine in it. Chevrolet had put that engine in the 1950's on a small scale, and then in the 1956's on a much larger scale. He quickly took on and outran everybody in town, which was an amazing feat to me. He was not well-liked around town after that, and he was probably glad when the telephone company sent him somewhere else to work because he would get the cold shoulder wherever he went.

1956 Ford Crown Victoria w/ 427 Cubic Inch

One of my friends in town, who was a little older than I, built a fine hot rod. My granddaddy and his dad were great friends. Granddaddy and he had worked together through the years with his daddy who owned and operated a garage and junkyard. He took a 1956 Ford two-door Crown Victoria and replaced the 272 cubic in. factory engine with a large block Ford FE engine. It was a 427 cubic inch behemoth. It was by far the fastest vehicle in town. It was a beautiful red color with the chrome integral roll bar (crown) going across the top of the vehicle behind the doors. He was a super mechanic, a skill he had learned from his daddy and from working in the junkyard and garage. After he joined the United States Marine Corps and left, his car stayed around town ending up being owned by another friend of mine in Surrency.

As you can tell there was not a tremendous amount of money in the budget for automobiles, but we all did as best we could. Some folks, who were either more talented, like the one

24

with the 1956 Crown Victoria, or those whose family had a little more money were able to get a newer, faster ride. Although I had one of the better paying jobs for a teenager, I made a whopping dollar and a quarter an hour. That was not sufficient to make a major automobile purchase.

My granddaddy was considered the best mechanic in the county during his day, and daddy was pretty good in his own right. He learned to be a mechanic working at his stepfather's garage in Bunnell, Florida. When he moved to Baxley he worked as a mechanic for the Chevrolet dealership. He told me that when he moved up to Baxley, he had tried to get granddaddy to go into business with him and for them to open up a garage, but my granddaddy did not like being tied down. He liked the flexibility of being able to relocate to a new job anytime his heart desired it. His customer base would follow him, because he had the reputation as being the best mechanic around. He liked to take a drink every once in a while, and when he was young he was a "bootlegger" during Prohibition. I have heard old timers say that they would rather have him work on their automobile drunk than anyone else sober. I have no doubt that had they been in the garage business when I was coming up, I most likely would have built something fast early. I am fairly skilled at mechanic work having rebuilt my Falcon transmission so many times. I have done numerous other mechanic jobs such as changing rear ends, replacing valve springs and the sort. But I know that if I had a garage at my disposal and two really good mechanics to rely upon, I would have built fast hot rods. There is no doubt my mind as to that. Daddy once told me that my Falcon was simple to work on. It is a fact that if I was able to work on it, it had to be relatively simple to work on. Daddy was not far off, and he was needed to assist on some of the items that required attention. I surely needed him to work on that thing with and for me.

1960 Ford Starliner

My friend, Jimmy, had a 1960 Ford Starliner with a 352 cubic inch police interceptor engine. It came equipped with automatic transmissions so it was not really great as a dragster but the thing would fly on top end. Like me he got into quite a bit of trouble for driving fast, and he even got in trouble for squealing tires. One night we were in Alma and had pulled off in front of the bus station and were talking. I was in my Falcon and had the cutouts off to make it sound bad. We sat there for a good while not noticing the city policeman hiding in the shadows back toward Waycross, Georgia. When we got ready to leave, we both took off together Jimmy burning rubber and me making a lot of racket. I was in front of Jimmy and saw the "Christmas Tree Lights" came on the patrol car. I threw my Falcon into neutral and shut the engine off so it would be quietened down and coasted into the lot by the cars for sale at the Ford dealership. Jimmy pulled into the filling station, jumped out and snatched hood up on the Starliner. He began beating something under there with his tire tool. When the policeman came up to him, he asked to borrow his flashlight. He beat and frammed around a little bit more and declared he might have it fixed. I had sidled up by them to see what was going on. Not to my surprise Jimmy was spinning a yarn to that policeman. He said that the garage was supposed to fix that accelerator linkage that very day, but they had lied to him. He apologized to the policeman because the car had just taken off, and he'd had to turn it off to get it in there and work on it. He thanked the policeman for the use of his flashlight and as he started to get in the car the policeman asked,

"What about those loud mufflers you got there boy" he asked.

"My mufflers aren't loud", replied Jimmy. "Listen".

He cranked the car up and revved it up and without the knowledge of the policeman, he slid the floor mat up on the accelerator causing the engine to rev up highly. He jumped back and grabbed the policeman's flashlight and beat and frammed up under the hood again, fussing the whole time.

The policeman agreed that his mufflers were not loud and told him to be careful on the way home with that bad accelerator.

I waited until the policeman was long gone before I cranked the Falcon up again. I was very careful not to make too much noise as I left Alma heading home.

Jimmy could come up with a story to fit any situation, and he got out of more things utilizing his quick brain to concoct a story that I think sometimes he even believed. So did a lot of policemen.

During that time, there were very few fast cars in our area. I remember the first Mustang that I ever saw was at the 1964 world's fair when I went there as a Boy Scout. I fell in love with mustangs then and there. The only large engines were in large family cars. They were not all in sports cars.

I had slowed down my street racing, due to the inherent risk of being caught by the law and fined heavily. I was beginning to race at the Claxton-Metter drag strip along with the Vidalia drag strip. I discovered that if you towed your car to the drag strip, like most people with the hot Gassers and Modified Productions did, they would pay you a tow fee of $25. I borrowed the tow bar from the Ford dealer and hooked my Falcon to the back of my 1951 International pickup truck. On the way home, near the little town of Mendes, I hit a big pothole on the top of the hill. I was unaware that it had torn the grips of the tow bar loose from the Falcon's front bumper. The impact of the washout had knocked the coil wire out of my truck, therefore it shut off. I felt the impact in the rear as the Falcon ran into the rear of the pickup truck and then watched as it careened off to the right, down the hill, through the ditch and hit head on into a humongous poplar tree. It then wrapped its lips around the tree in a giant hug. I saw the rear end of the Falcon fly up and slam back down at the time of impact. I knew I had screwed up. For a $25 tow fee, I had torn up my $695 Falcon.

Needless to say, my Falcon was totaled out and I was afoot again. I got the money from the insurance company and went to the local Savings and Loan to see what I might get in the way of a loan, so I could buy a new car. I really wanted one of those pretty 2 + 2 Fastback Mustangs like I had been seeing every once in a while.

1951 International Pickup

Bowers Collection

My 1951 International pickup was not the prettiest vehicle around nor was it technologically the most advanced. It was the one that daddy had acquired from his workplace and used to carry the Boy Scouts on campouts, but I drove it quite often. It was cool. I could gather up more girls in that ugly old black truck than in any vehicle I ever owned before or since. I remember one occasion when I was going to help one of the girls in school get a wooden coffin box from the local mortician to use in her talent portion of a beauty contest. She was going to do a pantomime scene to "I Want My Baby Back." We were going to use the pickup to haul it out to the school where she would use it in the contest. I went to her house and picked her up, and there was another girl there who wanted to go along. As we rode downtown more girls wanted to ride with us. I ended up sitting in the middle with six girls in the cab (one in my lap), and it was like I had died and gone to heaven with all those cute girls in there.

I could crank that truck up with it in first gear and shift every gear without using the clutch just by feathering the accelerator and playing with the RPM's. It had a worn-out shift tube so first gear to second gear was quite a long shift with the shift panel beyond top dead center after the shift.

We were always doing crazy (stupid) things like that. The old truck was tough.

Just to demonstrate how stupid teenagers can be, my friends and I would be driving down the road in that truck when I would open the door step out on the running board and let the one in the middle slip over under the wheel. I would then crawl into the back of the pickup around to the other side step on the running board open the door and get in on the shotgun side of the truck. We did not have a lot of common sense back then I guess it was due to being young there was a song "Be Young, Be Foolish, Be Happy" and I guess that's what we were because we were definitely young and foolish, and we were pretty happy with everything. Also, if you got the truck very fast the front fenders would flap like a buzzard trying to take off and fly because the fender struts were broken loose.

One of my cousins, Randall, and I were "Booger Chasers" as we tried to investigate every paranormal situation that we heard about. We were in the senior play in high school together and after play practice would go to cemeteries or maybe to Surrency, Georgia in order to find the famous Surrency Spook Light. We finally determined what the light was after being nearly scared out of our wits. I think it was the adrenaline rush that we craved that made us do these things. If you sat under the overpass on highway 341 at night you would see a light on the railroad track. It would start toward Odum and just would gain more and more intensity. It also would change colors from a reddish color to an orangish color and even a greenish color along with the brilliant white. As you would sit on the tracks wondering what it was, it suddenly disappeared. It was a great place to take a girl because a scared teenage girl would hold fast and tight to the boy she was with when encountering something like that. One night Randall and I walked down the railroad track toward it. We were apprehensive and did not know for sure what we were going to find but we were hell-bent to find the source. It was about 5 miles from the overpass to the City of Odum, Georgia. We walked all the way and discovered that highway 341 from Jesup, Georgia came into the middle of Odum at an angle. When a car approached the traffic signal in Odum (which accounted for the red, orange and green colors) the light would intensify dancing down the polished tops of the railroad track. After passing the intersection with the traffic light, the car truck headlights were blocked by a stand of timber. That is how we solved the mystery of the Surrency Spook Light.

It was a neat old truck that my cousin Billy and I used to rabbit hunt out of it, at night. I had loads of good times in that truck. About as many good times as I've ever had doing anything.

My 1966 Mustang 2 + 2 With Drag Trophies

Bowers Collection

Faster Cars

My 1966 2+2 Mustang

My first encounter seeing a Mustang was at the 1964 World's Fair in New York. I immediately fell in love with the little "Pony Car". I began to desire one at that time. It was "Love at First Sight".

A local schoolteacher had bought a 1964 ½ gold convertible Mustang with a black top. I thought it was really neat, and I guess it was at that point in time, I renewed my love affair with Ford's Mustang. I begin to really desire the ownership of one of those cool Mustangs. I went to the local dealer, who was my cousin, but could not find what I was looking for, which was a fastback (2+2). They did have a used GT 350H Shelby Mustang there, but I passed on it not knowing how bad it had been rawhided by the folks that rented it.

We were going to Bunnell, Florida, so I decided I would check the dealerships between my home and there. I went to talk with Mr. Oliver at the Savings and Loan, where I had a small savings account and we arranged for me to buy a car, if my parents would co-sign the note. I was new at this so I did not have a clue about financing a car. I had paid cash money for the Falcon (instead of going on the senior class trip) but a new Mustang was going cost a tremendous amount more than that Falcon. Maybe as much is three times as much or even more than that.

Back to my dilemma of being afoot. I looked at the Ford dealerships around home and did not find anything that I really liked that was priced in the range that I wanted to pay. We were going to Flagler Beach, Florida for a vacation so I looked at every Ford dealership between Baxley and Bunnell, Florida. I found nothing in Blackshear, Folkston, Callahan, St. Augustine or Jacksonville that really interested me because I had it in my heart's desire to have fastback and all I could find was coupes and convertibles. The next morning, I went to the Ford dealership in Burnell, Florida that was owned by some family friends, and sat down and talked with the owner, Harry. I told him what I wanted but that I didn't find anything on his lot to fill that need.

He took some papers out of his desk and said, "I have one coming in, but I don't know when it'll be here."

Just about the time he was saying that a car transport pulled up in his lot. On the back of that transport was a Wimbledon White 1966 2+2 Mustang. I asked if that was it. He said he didn't know but it could be because it was the right color. After further checking he confirmed that in fact was his and it would be unloaded shortly. I sat down with him and asked him how much he had to have in cash money. I had heard that sometimes made a difference, but I really had no experience in car buying. He scratched some figures and said he would take $2400 cash. We made the deal, and he said he would have it ready by noon. I went back to retrieve my parents. We went up there together, and we wrote out the check that the banker had said to write, and he would cover it when we got back, which he did.

I went to Daytona Beach that night, and as soon as I crossed the Main Street bridge, I pulled over to talk with two girls who were walking toward the beach. We talked a little and they were impressed with my Mustang and hopped in the car, to ride with me. The Mustang had already attracted some girls, which was a bonus. We rode up and down on Daytona Beach and I was sure that my new ride was the prettiest car there.

I became a hit with the pretty fastback Mustang. The 200 horsepower that the engine produced was far more than the 85 horsepower that my Falcon had produced, and it took some getting used to the difference in power. The main difference was the takeoff. The RPM's could not be too high or wheel spin would occur. I had to listen to the engine with my ear since at the time I had no tachometer in order to be consistent with the takeoff. I practiced for a while taking off and running through the gears until I was fairly consistent.

It was not long before I was challenged to a drag race to which I obliged. It was equipped with a floor shift 3 speed transmission. I found out that with the extremely high gearing in the rear end that I could go completely through the quarter mile in second gear. It being a hydraulic lifter equipped 289 with a two-barrel carburetor it was not extremely fast. The rear end was a 2.80 to 1, which was extremely high. I did find it to be beneficial that I only had one gearshift to contend with. That meant that I only had one chance of making a mistake shifting gears. Most folks at least had two and people with a four-speed had three. Finally, I purchased a tachometer and installed it so I could be consistent with the RPM's at the start and at the shift points. The 289 with hydraulic lifters was notorious because it would float the valves at about 5000 RPM's, and the lifters would pump up and the engine would shake like "a dog trying to pass a peach seed." I tried to tie my shifts at 4900 RPM's to maximize my horsepower. There had become quite a few folks with 289 Mustangs around town. None of which had any more than a four-barrel carburetor. No one around town had a High-performance 289's, so the racing was fairly even.

I started taking my Mustang to the drag strip on Sundays and began to run pretty well in my class. The extra weight of the fastback caused it to run in one class higher than the coupes. The little white Mustang would run the quarter mile in the mid-fourteens which was respectable. I learned by power shifting instead of speed shifting it would keep the RPM's up and cause you to turn a faster elapsed time. Although I wasn't fast compared to some of the muscle cars that were around home in the 1965 and 1966 era. I was consistent enough that if they wanted to race me, I would be glad to oblige them because I was supposed to lose anyway, but if they made one mistake, I would beat them. I purchased an 8000 RPM's tachometer and installed it on my dashboard. At 5000 RPM's the valves would still float on that 289 and pump up. I was careful not to rev beyond 4900 RPM's so as to get the maximum performance out of the car. There are two types of shifting used in racing. One is the speed shift where the feet shuffled on the accelerator and clutch and the shift is timed perfectly. That is called speed shifting. A power shift is when the accelerator foot never leaves the floor, and the shift is made in conjunction with "fanning" the clutch pedal. Fortunately for me the Ford clutch would let out about three quarters of an inch from the top. Chevrolet clutches let out farther down which always made it difficult for me to speed shift or power shift a General Motors product. Throughout the next several years my proficiency at "power shifting" most likely made the difference in several races, due to the fact that the RPM's would not drop during a "power shift" operation.

I read in one of the car magazines that you could replace the valve springs and retainers on a 289 hydraulic lifted engine, with the springs and retainers to fit the 289 high-performance (which came equipped with solid lifters), and that two things would occur. Number one you could rev up the engine to somewhere in the neighborhood of 6000 RPM's before the valves would float. The stronger springs would cause the engine to recover quicker, and the valves would not pump up. I went to the Ford dealership. By this time, I knew their books almost as well as they did, so I looked up the parts and asked them to order them for me. When they came in, my daddy built an adapter to screw into the spark plug hole in the shop that he supervised at work and it keep the lifter raised with compressed air. He, Billy and I changed them out as shade tree mechanics. I was careful to torque all of the springs down correctly and was again lucky that my valve cover gaskets didn't tear, so I didn't even have to buy new ones. I did this for a little over ten dollars.

I took the Mustang out on the road and sure enough you could wind at the 6000 RPM's, and when the valves floated, if I could shift quickly the engine would recover immediately. This was going to be a big boom for me. I had just added to my car what it would take to overcome the two extra barrels that some folks had in their Mustang carburetors. I took advantage of it and I, for a short period of time, could not find a Mustang with a 289 four-barrel that wanted to race me.

A friend of mine, who was younger and played in the high school band with me, had a pretty Burnt Amber Mustang. It was also a 289 cubic inch two-barrel and ran something close to what mine did before the alteration. I took him to ride one day out toward Surrency. I asked him how much his Mustang would turn. He replied that it would turn about 5000 to 5100 RPM's before it would float the valves. I told him to watch my tachometer, and I got down on the "Little White Stallion". The RPM's quickly climbed beyond 5000 RPM and when they hit 5900 RPM, I shifted into second year. I went a little way and turned around and headed back to town and my buddy, Billy, had not said a word. When I went to let him out at his car, he asked me why mine would turn so many RPM's. I told him I thought that they all would turn that much, because mine always had, lying through my teeth. He walked away shaking his head and mumbling something that I could not hear.

On one Sunday my friends Billy and Wink were with me at the Vidalia strip. Billy had always had a knack for making cars run fast, and he asked if I would like to cut .10 of a second off my elapsed time, which was a no-brainer. I said, "of course". He dove under the hood and took my fan off, unplugged my generator, increased the air pressure in my front tires to 50 pounds and decreased my rear tires to 18 pounds. Much to my amazement it did cut more than one tenth of a second off my time. It is amazing what little things can do.

After getting used to my little white Mustang, my cousin Lamar challenged me to a race. We went out to the "barrel" which was one of our favorite places to race and turned them on. I won handily, which did not make Lamar happy. You have to understand he and I carried some of the same competitive genes, and neither one of us liked to lose. Our competitive spirit pushed us as children on the baseball field, playing marbles, at the swimming pool and

37

especially on pinball machines.   Later it translated to the pool table. Lamar was very athletic and was a good runner. He was one of the faster runners in school as opposed to his slower cousin Bill. We were both baseball players and in High School we both lettered for four years

I had been going to night classes at the University of Georgia off-campus in Waycross. One night while returning home I stopped in Alma at the filling station located at the Ford dealership, to get gasoline and a coke. The attendant asked if mine was the fast Mustang from Baxley to which I replied, "No, mine is probably the slowest since it's only a two-barrel and is heavier than the sedan Mustangs."

"Whoever the owner of that fast Mustang from Baxley is, he will have to watch out." He smugly stated, "There's a guy in the back with the red Mercury, souping it up to surprise the fellow with the fast one!"

I didn't know but one red Mercury that would be getting souped up, and I immediately knew who's the Mustang was. After getting gas, I pulled around to the side and parked. I walked in without being noticed and saw that they had the cylinder heads off Lamar's engine.

"Did you tear it up Lamar?", I inquired.

Lamar had the funniest look on his face when he turned and saw me standing behind the car. He looked like the kid who had gotten caught with his hand in the cookie jar. He stuttered and stammered but was unable to explain to me what was happening and what he was doing. I later found out he had the man to put a cam in it and added solid lifters in order to make it turn a little better. That didn't make any difference, I still outran him.

1967 Oldsmobile 442

Later Lamar got an Oldsmobile 442 that was Gold colored. It was quick but was a departure from the original 442 (4 Barrel – 4 Speed – 2 exhaust pipes). It was equipped with a 400 cubic inch engine with a 4-barrel Rochester carburetor, with an automatic transmission. It would run the quarter mile in the high fourteens and low fifteens.

There was one occasion when Lamar was racing a boy that owned a 383 Dodge. We went out Zoar Road to one of our drag strips so that they could turn it on. For some reason I ended up as the passenger in the Dodge rather than in Lamar's car. Just as we were completing the drag race local sheriff's department had "Wolf Packed Us." They had all three of the sheriff and deputy cars converge upon the spot at once. I believe that someone had most likely ratted us out.

The boy who was driving the Dodge I was in had no earthly idea where he was because he was from the other side of the county. I was directing him on where to go and we hit a dirt road so that I could make sure that we "Dusted" the law car that was following us which would impede their vision. As we approached a T intersection, I told him to get ready to hit the brakes and turn left when I told him. I did and he did. The sheriff who was in pursuit behind us did not negotiate the turn but went out through the pines happens in front of the T intersection. The boy was afraid to bring me back to town, so he let me out of his car at Pine Forest subdivision. I had to walk in. When I got to Shannon Lightsey's station I needed something cold to drink because a German Shepherd had gotten after me in Weatherly Park causing me to run most of the way to Lightsey's. After a brief respite, I walked on to the Tastee Freeze where my car was parked. When I got there, I was told that the sheriff had picked Lamar up at the Tastee Freeze. I noticed Lamar's car was parked there.

I waited for them to return Lamar to his car before I went home. When they brought him back, he and I talked briefly and he said that the sheriff is asking lots of questions that he had not confessed to anything. That was good because I was hopeful I did not get implicated in all of this hullabaloo.

When Lamar left to go home, I cranked up my Mustang and headed to my house. Like an idiot, instead of taking the back roads I went straight up town to the main traffic light at US 1 and US 341. The problem was that was where the Sheriff's office was located. As I stopped for the traffic light, I heard the Sheriff holler for me to come over there. I obliged and pulled in at the Sheriff's office.

The sheriff began to interrogate me but made a mistake of saying we don't know for fact that you were there we just want you to confess. I've done a lot of stupid things in my life but I was not about to confess to something that he had no proof of so I told him I wasn't even sure what he was talking about. His name was

"Red" Carter, and his face turned blood red trying to get me to confess. After a while I informed him that he had kept me up there past the time that I was supposed to be at home. I knew my parents would give me the devil for being late so I asked him if he was going to call them and tell them that he had detained me for no good reason. Shaking his head he told me to go and get out of there. I jumped in my Mustang and headed to the house.

I understood the next day that the boy that owned the Dodge, who worked at Piggly Wiggly, was questioned by him also. I believe that someone ratted us out, but I don't know who. Nothing else ever came of it because I guess since Lamar, Wade nor I confess to anything it was dropped.

One night, while trying to avoid capture by the local law, I made the 20 mile trip from Baxley to Alma in 9 ½ minutes in my Mustang, only to be captured by a roadblock in Alma. That was the night when I learned that you could not outrun the General Electric overdrive that was mounted under the dash of those police cars. That signal travels at the speed of 186,000 feet per second, which was much more speed than my 1966 Mustang could muster. I learned my lesson that night and never again, when being pursued, did I run in a straight line. From then on, I would take turns to the left and then to the right to avoid any predictability on their part. After that, when I chose to flee, I was never again captured. Although on a few occasions I was smart enough to see the futility of trying to run and just pulled over and accepted my just due. Those were all expensive decisions, but, in every case, I knew I would be found out and captured regardless.

There was one time, though, when I was "squealing my wheels" in downtown Baxley and the local police fell in behind me. I was not far from the house, so I quickly pulled up in the front yard and left the car running as I ran into the house. Several minutes later I emerged the front door to find the Baxley City Police car still there parked behind my Mustang.

As I approached the police cruiser I stated "Man! I almost didn't make it! That was about as close as you could come without getting into trouble and being embarrassed!"

The policeman had a puzzled look on his expression for he knew that I had not avoided trouble because they were sitting there waiting for me.

"What do you mean?" One of the policemen asked.

I replied, taking a play out of my buddy Jimmy's playbook, "My stomach is tore up and I like to have made a mess in my car. I got here just in time to keep that from happening."

The policemen still looked puzzled and they were shaking their heads as they put the cruiser in reverse to back up and pull out on to the road. One of those policeman I would later see from time to time, after he had retired from the force. The first question he would ask was how my stomach was doing. I am sure he knew I was lying but I guess I was so innovative with the lie that they let me go.

Neal, who was a longtime friend, was in the Army. He had come to Baxley to visit his aunt who he had lived with while in High School. His father had owned Bunnell Motor Company, which was a Ford dealership. His brother, Harry, owned it when I bought the 1966 Mustang from him. Neal, Winkie and I went to a night club in Jesup one night. Neal got so rowdy, challenging some pulpwooders in that place. I knew we had to get him out of there quickly, lest we get embroiled in a fight we could not win. We were outnumbered at least four to one.

When we got back home, he said that if we went to Ocala with him, he would introduce us to some girls that he knew there. That was all it took so we left in his car at 11 o'clock in the evening. We spent the weekend in Ocala, and as we started home, we heard on the radio about a dragstrip that was opening in Gainesville. We decided to go to the new strip. When we got there, we found that it was the first races that track was having. The grand opening would be the next weekend.

At first, I was content to just sit in the stands. As the cars were lining up for practice, I got the urge to race. We were in Neal's 1966 Galaxy with a 260 cubic inch small block V-8 in it. I took the keys and entered the car in the race. They asked how I wanted to compete, and I chose the stock class. They were having what they called bracket racing, which I knew nothing of.

In the practice, I found the Galaxy was a "dog". I did get to race a practice run against the Harris Brothers' record holding Corvette. I beat him about the first foot or two out of the hole, but then he blew my doors off. The track was a mile long made of new asphaltic concrete with 4 turnoff lanes to return to the pits. It was an awesome track. The finest I ever saw or raced on. I won my class but discovered that the bracket racing was where I needed to be, since I could run consistent times. There was a Volkswagen beetle that won the championship and some pretty good prize money. His elapsed time was 21.30 seconds, and he was spotted so much against the other cars that he was racing against they would "Break Out" trying to catch him and would lose. Since I was pretty consistent, I might have gone a long way in that type of competition. I also got to see Linda Vaughn, Miss Hurst Shifter that day. Man was she pretty!

That day I saw a Mustang with a 300 cubic inch straight six that ran like a "Bat Out of Hell". The match race there that day was that Mustang from Tennessee against a 1940 Willis Coupe Gasser. It was a fine match with the Mustang winning 3 of the 5 races, in the last race when they were tied two to two.

On Sunday nights when I returned from the drag strip. I would circle the Tastee Freeze. All the boys with the fast Chevelles would be backed into the parking places and as I came by, with my classification still on my windshield they would challenge me to races. Let me reiterate, I was not scared of any of them, and I would race any of them although, most of the time, it was a futile effort. When I was competing a 200 horsepower engine up against a 325 horsepower engine, I didn't have much of a chance. The one saving grace was the fact that I only had one shift to make in the quarter mile and I could get off the line exceptionally well. Therefore, they had better not spin down on the start or miss a shift, because the difference in our ET's was less than one half second and that is not very long. I mostly lost when racing the higher powered cars, but I was supposed to. Anytime they screwed up and I beat them it was something to swell up about. I was not afraid to race any of them, at any time, because I wasn't going to screw up and they might.

Finally, one Sunday night I had had it, all the way to full, and did not want to hear their challenges anymore. I walked up to a group of them who were mocking my Mustang and challenging me to drag race, and I made a small announcement to the group.

"I'm going to get me a Ford that is so fast that when I circle the Tastee Freeze, the fenders on the Chevrolets are gonna quiver with fear, and hope that I don't call any of you out." I announced.

They all laughed but I began looking for a faster car.

That search included almost buying a GT 350 H mustang and a beautiful white 1967 427 cubic inch Cobra.

1966 GT 350 H Shelby Mustang

1967 427 Cu. In. Shelby Cobra

1968 ½ 428 Cobra Jet Mustang

The Ford dealership had gotten in a Mustang GT 350H (that was a GT 350 made especially by Caroll Shelby for Hertz rental cars) it was a 289 high performance that had been taken one more step, as had all GT 350's, by Caroll Shelby and the horsepower had increased from 271 to 306. I could not get together with the folks at the Ford dealership because they wanted way too much for a used car and I knew what a GT 350 cost new. I kept looking. On another occasion the Ford dealership had a Galaxy 500 with a 427 cubic inch engine with two 4-barrel carburetor's producing 425 hp. As I tried to deal with them, a friend of mine, who was a drag racer from Glenville, came and bought the car out from under me. I seriously considered a 427 cubic inch 425 hp Cobra in Daytona Beach, Florida at the price of $7995.00.

Finally in early 1968 Ford had announced that they would produce a limited number of Mustangs with a 427 cubic inch engine. The engine would be a single four-barrel model with 410 hp. I tried to check up on my finances and found that I could afford one. I went to the Ford dealership to order one of those big bad Mustangs. I was informed that Ford had sold the three-hundred 427 cubic inch Mustangs that were planned and would produce no more (although I did later find a 427 Cougar that was not for sale). These were detuned 427 cubic inch engines, and I am glad that I didn't get one because it would've taken more work to make it faster. I found out though, that they were going to produce a 428 cubic inch model later in the year. This engine was going to be faster than the 428 cubic inch police interceptor for a couple reasons. Number one, was the fact that it would have Series 1, 427 heads. Number two, it would have a larger Holley carburetor (735 cubic foot per minute, dual inlet Holly). Number three, it would have a less restrictive exhaust system with a type of factory headers. Number four was the Ram Air Package based on a vacuum activated hood scoop. They chose to call these cars Cobra Jets. As a side note both the 427 cubic inch and the 428 cubic inch were offshoots of the old 406 cubic inch (4.13 bore 3.78 stroke). With the 427 cubic inch the bore was increased from 4.13 to 4.23 and on the 428 cubic inch the bore remained the same but the stroke was increased to 3.98. The 427 cubic inch should rev quicker and the 428 cubic inch should have made more torque.

The Ford dealer and I talked about the price for the 428 cubic inch Mustang. and I told him I wanted it. They said they would order it. We had agreed on a price of $4000 deducting the trade-in value of my white 1966 Mustang but when the new Mustang arrived in May they wanted 300 more dollars for it than we had agreed upon. It didn't seem fair to me so I, as disappointed as I was, told them that I was not interested. As I would ride by the Ford dealership and look into the window of the main showroom, that pretty Sunlit Gold Mustang would call out to me, but the Scottish blood in me refused to pay that much extra. After about two weeks the dealer called me and said that I could have it for the $4000 if I still wanted it. I went back to the dealership and we consummated the deal on the 1968 1/2 428 Cobra Jet Mustang coupe. Now if you think that transitioning from 85 horsepower to 200 horsepower was bad transitioning from 200 horsepower to over 400 horsepower was worse. Although the horsepower was rated at 335 for insurance purposes, all accounts that I have read was that it had 410.

The 428 cubic inch engine was equipped with series 1, 427 heads. A Holley 735 C F M, dual inlet carburetor sat atop the medium rise intake. It came equipped with a Hollman and Moody 11 1/2 inch diaphragm clutch and Ford's bulletproof top loader, close ratio four speed transmission. It also came equipped with a ram air package with a functional hood scoop, governed by the amount of vacuum you pulled, which would drop open and force the air directly into the carburetor when the performance needed it. On top of that the car came stock with a Ford 9 inch traction lock rear end, Shelby road race suspension and Goodyear Polyglass tires. The Mustang also came equipped with disc brakes and Ford's first antilock braking system. I was not pleased with the vacuum linkage which waited for 4500 RPM to open the back two barrels. I visited a friend that raced Fords and he told me to remove the vacuum linkage cover. There I would find a spring and ball bearing. He said to remove them throwing the ball as far in the woods and clip one coil from the spring. The back two barrels would open immediately.

That car was the fastest thing that I had ever been behind the wheel of. It took me about two weeks to get used to it with many trips out to the desolate roads in the county, learning how to take off without spinning down and practicing going through the gears. I didn't challenge anybody at home to a race because I was not used to the car and they didn't challenge me because they were unsure to what I had. Finally, after about two weeks I was confident that I could take off without spinning down. The most efficient way I could do it was to rev it to 1800 RPM and slip the clutch off, feeling the traction or loss of traction as I would go. Once I got it in motion then I would shift the gears at 6800 RPM, utilizing a power shift. My greatest problem with the car was getting it from a standing start into motion without spinning down and losing valuable time. Only my friends Billy and Wink knew how fast the car was since they would ride with me in these practice sessions. They both declared that it was fast, but since I had not had it up alongside anybody else, I didn't know, relatively, how fast it was. The speedometer registered 120 mph, and I could run out of numbers in third gear. There was an odometer post dead center in the bottom of the speedometer, and I could make the speedometer needle strike that post three times. On the third time it would stay there. At that point in time in high gear I was turning 6700 RPM's. Billy and I measured a mile course and took a stopwatch, we timed it in the flying mile. Billy calculated the speed to be 152 ½ miles an hour which was faster than I've ever been in my life. He also calculated the RPM using the circumference of the tire which bore out the 152 miles an hour speed. The car also had Ford's first antilock braking system on the front, and you could panic stop at 150 miles an hour and the tires would not lock up in the last 10 feet of the stop. Billy later purchased a 1969 Camaro, with four-wheel disc brakes, that would stop even faster (I swore that the paint would slide forward on his when he stopped).

Since I bought the car in the middle of June, the July fourth weekend was coming up, and I decided to make my annual trek to Daytona International Speedway for the fourth of July races. I especially liked the format they had where at midnight they would run the Paul Revere 250, which was sports cars race on the road racecourse inside the trioval. It started at midnight and raced until they had gone 250 miles. The stars of the show were the Mustangs, the Camaros, the Cougars, and the Firebirds. These vehicles sported big V-8 engines and sounded good when they ran the portion that included the trioval. I liked to sit on the number nine turn, where they would come off the inside flat track and hit the banked number two turn on the trioval.

49

I headed out to Florida to get with my cousins, Henry and Hutch. As I came into Jacksonville, on US 1, where the four-lane started, there was a series of traffic lights. Now you must understand the only thing on that Mustang that denoted that it was a Cobra Jet was the hood scoop and a flat black stripe that went up the length of the hood to the windshield. I pulled up at the first traffic light, there was a 1966 GT Mustang (the GT's came equipped with a 289 cubic inch and a four-barrel carburetor). He had his cutouts loose and was revving his engine up in a challenge to me. As we awaited the light, I eased my RPM's up to about 1500, and when the light changed, he took off with all he had. I matched acceleration with him, without straining and just beat him as we came to the next traffic light. He revved his engine up again and I followed suit. When the light changed, I did just like I had at the last light. I just managed to stay just a little bit ahead of him but never put my Cobra Jet in a strain. We came to the third light, I had enjoyed about as much of him as I could stand. When He revved his engine up, I revved of mine up to 1800 and when the light changed, I poured the coal to the little Cobra Jet and left him in my dust. In the quarter mile I must have outrun him 20 car lengths or better. The next light was green, but I pulled up and stopped and I waited for it to turn red and waited for him to pull up alongside me.

He rolled down his window and asked, "What in the hell do you have in there?"

To which I replied "Four-two-eight!"

He was still cussing the last time I saw him.

I arrived in Bunnell, and Henry was beside himself with my new acquisition. He looked it over from one side to the other. The Sunlit Gold Cobra Jet was one beautiful automobile. It just looked mean sitting there. As I stated earlier, in addition to all of the performance equipment in the running gear it was equipped with a Ford 9 inch, (Traction Lock) 3.50 to 1 differential, Goodyear Polyglass tires and a Shelby road race suspension. The tachometer registered 8000 RPM and sat beside the 120 mile an hour speedometer in the instrument panel.

1968 Sunlit Gold 428 Cobra Jet Coupe Mustang

IHRA Night Nationals

(Near World Record Run)

We went to the Paul Revere 250 and the Firecracker 400 and thoroughly enjoyed them, especially since a Ford won it. And while we were there, we learned of IHRA Night Nationals to be held at the Samsula Airport, near Daytona Beach. We immediately made plans to take the Cobra Jet to the dragstrip, so we could know what kind of elapsed time range it would run. Upon exiting Daytona International Speedway, we went out the exit over the back straightaway and it was all I could do to keep that Mustang from turning left and trying out the back straightaway and number three and four turns.

The next day we showed up at the airport and I classified my Mustang. Since I didn't say anything about what was in it and I did not know what class it was supposed to be in. They put me in C Pure Stock. I thought I had snuck in as a 390 cubic inch engine. We went back to the pits. Henry, Hutch and I prepared to race. I was informed that in pure stock I couldn't even take off my hubcaps, or breather or anything else so I obliged. In the time trials it took me a little while to get used to starting on a concrete surface rather than asphaltic concrete surface. It only took a couple of runs and I was used to it and then I started looking for cars like the ones that were owned by the boys back at home and were parked in the Tastee Freeze parking lot. I outgunned all of the types 396 Chevelles, GTOs, 442's, Street Hemi Barracudas and Plymouth Furys, 440 cubic inch Mopars and even whipped a 427 Corvette and a GT 500 Shelby Mustang (which had a 428 cubic inch police interceptor in it). I could have gone home then, because I knew how my car stacked up against all the competition back home, but they gave the call that the class eliminations were starting.

In my first run in the class eliminations, I was pitted against a 360 horsepower GTO. As we moved up and my nose hit the pre-stage light, they instructed us to shut the engine off. I rolled down the window to determine what was going on.

I heard the man on the PA system announce.

"In the left lane we have a brand-new 1968 ½ 428 Cobra Jet Mustang. This is the first one that we have seen. Since they haven't been out a month, it's a good bet it will be the first one that you will see. Now is your chance to see if they run well and live up to all the hype."

I wish he had not done that, for my head had begun to swell. That didn't do anything for my concentration in the race. We staged and the Christmas tree lights came down. We both took off. I took off too hot and began to spin too much, allowing him to get a lead on me. I shifted to second gear early, in order to break the loss of traction. I overcame him in second gear and when I hit third gear, which was my killer gear, I left him several car lengths in arrears. I breathed a sigh of relief because I had almost screwed up by not paying attention and doing what I was supposed to.

The next run was against a Chevelle and I got off just fine. It felt good and I shifted from third to fourth just as I was crossing the quarter mile. I could have stretched it beyond 6800 RPM, but was afraid to push it farther, so I executed the power shift just as I broke the lights. When I got back to the pits, Henry and Hutch were jumping up and down. Wondering what had gotten into them, I pulled up and rolled the window down. Henry quickly informed me that the man on the PA had said that I had turned a 12.83 elapsed time at a speed of 127 miles an hour and that the world record for the class was 12.80. He further said that if I could break the record and back it up to within 10 percent, I would be the owner of the new world record.

I didn't even have a tire gauge, much less an air tank where I could have done some of what my friend Billy had taught me. No telling what I could have done if I had 55 pounds of air in the front tires and 18 in the back tires. I turned 12.83 five more times that night and never could break the 12.80 mark. I went on to win C Pure Stock and Pure Stock Eliminator. As we raced for Street Eliminator, I eliminated everyone in my path until it was just me and one 396 Chevelle left.

We were having to spot the differences in the world record for the classes so I had to spot him .47 of a second. I know that does not sound like much, but it felt like an eternity to me. It looked like I had given him several days head start before my light came down. I took off and ran the very best race I could. When we crossed the 132 foot stripe from the end and broke the lights which started timing the speed, I was at his back bumper, coming on fast. When we crossed the stripe at the end of the quarter mile, he had me about a foot which was extremely disappointing to me because I would've liked to have taken all the hardware home with me that night. I later learned that he was the world record holder for his class and that I had run 12.83 one more time in my attempt to whip him and he had run right on his record for his class.

To add insult to injury, as we were coming out of the airport that night, someone had removed the barricades that showed where you made the turns onto the different runways leaving only black creosote post and three strands of barbed wire against the background of black asphalt. I never saw the fence until the post came through the windshield and popped just to the right of my right ear. Hutch, who had just been in a wreck not many days earlier, hollered "not again!"

The state trooper who worked accident would not let me drive the car home although it was only cosmetic damage to it. He said I would have to have a wrecker. I told him that I had a good friend, Bono, with a wrecker service in Bunnell, which was where I was taking it anyway and asked if we could call him.

He said, "No I'll get you the wrecker I want you to have."

I had to pay the wrecker operator $75.00, in cash money, before he would drop the car in Uncle Gene's yard. I had to borrow the money from Aunt Myra, because I didn't have that much on me. Although I had good insurance, Allstate at the time, he would have no part of filing an insurance claim.

It took some finagling to get the Florida State Troopers to allow me to drive my car home with a hole in the windshield. Thank God my Aunt Virginia was good friends with a Captain of the Florida State Troopers. She both got me permission to tape around the edges of the windshield and drive home. She informed him of the actions of the state trooper that worked the case. I don't know if he got into trouble, but I do believe he was getting a kickback and I hope he did, in fact, get into trouble.

Back Home

When I returned home, I had to get the car repaired with front end damaged and the windshield to be replaced. That didn't take too long, and I was back driving my Cobra Jet around town. I had confidence now that the Cobra Jet would handle anything I was aware of that was driving on the streets around home. There were some "track only cars" that I did not know whether or not I could stand up to, but I had no doubts that I could handle anything that was running on the streets based upon the 12.83 elapsed time at Daytona. I had also perfected my "clutch slipping" starts with street tires.

Some friends of mine, two brothers "Squeak" and "Little Bit" were known to have some of the faster cars in the county during that point in time. "Squeak' had a beautiful black Chevrolet Impala that would really run, and "Little Bit" had a blue Chevelle that was pretty fast also. "Squeak" and I both worked for the same governmental agency, and I spotted him uptown one afternoon. I asked him to hop in and take a ride with me. He obliged and we started out US 1 South of town. I was in high gear running about 50 mph when we cleared the city limits sign. The vacuum linkage on that 735 CFM Holly was set so that the back two barrels did not open up until enough vacuum was pulled which was at about 4500 RPM. I pushed the pedal to the floor and the back two carburetor barrels opened up. When it did, there was such a surge of acceleration that it really felt like an automatic transmission hitting passing gear. I held the accelerator down until we reached about 120 mph, before I let off. "Squeak" looked at me funny and told me that he was surprised, because he was sure that I had a four-speed transmission but it felt like I had hit passing gear with an automatic. Then I came to a complete stop and took off slipping the clutch to avoid spinning. I revved it up to 6800 in first gear, before power-shifting into the second. I repeated that in second gear and third gear. The whole time I was accelerating, "Squeak" was pinned to the seat. I turned around and started back for town. He told me he believed that it was the fastest car he'd ever been in. He had heard of acceleration pinning you to the seat where you could not take a $100 bill taped to the dash off but he had never experienced it until then. Getting "Squeak's" stamp of approval was plenty good for me.

Once while I was at work, my boss called and instructed me to check on the utilities operation on U. S. 1 South of town. Instead of taking the company vehicle, I elected to take my brand-new Mustang. One of the other employees, James, decided he would ride with me. As I hit the city limits, I gunned it. After running through the gears, I had reached a speed of about 130 miles per hour as I approached the worksite. I had to get on disc brakes in order to slow it down in time to turn off to check on the work that was going on. I had glanced over at James in the passenger seat, and it was easy to detect the fear in his eyes. He had not said a word but was holding on for all he was worth. He would not ride back to the office with me but instead went to a house nearby and called for someone else to come get him. I fear that I scared him just a little bit too much with the raw power of this C J 428. He never again got in the car with me, and I could not understand why because I was a good driver.

I did not like the vacuum linkage on the Mustang, because you would have to hit 4500 RPM's before the back two barrels would drop open. I had a friend in a neighboring town that had been a drag racer and actually was working for Ford Motor

Company out of Jacksonville at the time. I went to his house and told him of my difficulty with the carburetor. He told me to take the plate off my vacuum linkage on the side of the carburetor. In there he told me I would find a coiled spring and a ball bearing. He told me to throw that ball bearing into the woods just as far as I could and to clip one coil off that spring and replace it back under the plate. I did that and went out to test it. When my foot would hit the floorboard, the back two barrels of the carburetor would immediately open giving that thirsty engine a large swallow of gasoline.

After that, Billy took the check plug out of the top and adjusted it so that when you shook the car, gasoline would slosh out of the carburetor. It would actually feed so much gas at a dead stop that if you were standing behind the car the raw gas would almost blind you. It only took it only a little while and that 428 was taking everything that carburetor could give it. It made the carburetor react as if it had mechanical linkage, instead of vacuum linkage. That pleased me greatly, for I then felt as though I had the full benefit of a four-barrel carburetor when that 735 cubic foot a minute Holley would open up and begin to moan. (A sound I still love to hear is that distinct Holley moan). Billy and I then took the smog pump off and took all the "Smog Plumbing" off and plug the holes with short bolts. We also changed from a single point distributor to a dual point. That was the extent of all that we ever had to do to that Mustang to make it run.

I often wondered if the CJ engine could take all the gasoline that a 935 CFM Holly could pump.

One evening Billy, his brother Leon and I were returning from a neighboring town in the "Gold Jet". It had been misting rain, and highway 341 had a light film of moisture on its surface.

We were running along at about sixty miles per hour. Thankfully the traffic was light that evening.

Out of nowhere Leon remarked, "Do you think it would spin if you got down on it?"

Without thinking I "fanned the clutch" and slammed the accelerator to the floor. The car immediately lost traction and began to spin around in the middle of the highway. After about three circles I was able to regain control without leaving the highway "or wrecking". I was "shaking like a dog trying to pass a peach seed" when I corralled the Mustang, I got my speed down to about fifty miles per hour and looked back at Leon.

"Don't ever say anything like that again", I said in a shaky voice, "I don't have enough sense to not listen to you!"

I never tried that again out of respect for the raw power of the 428.

I kept that "bad boy" for over a year. I only lost three heads-up races during that timeframe.

The first time was at the Savannah Dragway, where one of the few times in my life I "slept on the lights". I was at the time racing a hot Z-28 Camaro for the class championship. Due to my error, he jumped me 6 to 8 car links on the start.

I was in catch-up mode. I almost spun down trying to recover from my mistake but finally got all that horsepower corralled up and began tracking him down. This was another case where I made up almost a full car length, in the last 132 feet. He beat me by less than a foot and my friends in the pits said that the PA announcer's statement was "The fastest one slept". My elapsed time was better than his, but my reaction time killed me. I went to him after the races when the grudge races were going on and offered to race him again and would bet $50 against that trophy he had just won. He refused.

The second time was when I was racing a good friend of mine from Alma who had a 440 Dodge RT. We were fairly even as we took off, which was a rarity for me, since I had to slip the clutch at 1800 RPM, in order to get a clean start. When I power shifted to second gear, the clutch pedal did not return from the floor. I quickly let off the accelerator in order to keep from blowing up my baby. He won the race. We later raced after I got the clutch checked out, finding that sometimes diaphragm clutches will stick, and I outran him handily. This time I outran him something like eight or nine car links.

The third time was in a race with a good friend of mine who had a 64 Chevelle. He had just had the engine cammed-up and had it balanced and blue-printed. It was a beast. We ran on a surface treatment road (which is not asphaltic concrete but bare rock on liquid asphalt) in the county. I did not get off well. I must've been excited, because I came out a little hot, and again had to shift early to break the spin. Meantime, with cheater slicks on, he had jumped me several car links, because he had made an excellent start. Just as we passed the quarter mile, I passed him, but he had me in the quarter. My mistake could cost me dearly although I did not mind getting beaten by a friend, but I did mind getting beaten by a Chevrolet. Billy and I had measured the quarter mile exactly with a steel tape at that location. Our precision may have cost me bragging rights because if that stripe had not been painted all the way across the road my buddy might not have known where the quarter ended. There may have been some question about who the winner was. Billy and I both liked to be pretty precise about what we did and, in that case, it cost me.

Trip to Louisiana

I was dating a girl who decided to go to college at Louisiana Tech, which is located in the Northwest area of Louisiana in Ruston. It'd been a while since I'd seen her, so I decided to take off some time from work and pay her a visit. I worked until 5 o'clock that Friday afternoon and went home. I ate, showered and "headed west young man". I had never been any further west than Columbus, Georgia or Phoenix City, Alabama as an adult. I was heading into unknown territory. I drove to Columbus and hit US 80. I 20 was in the process of being built but was only open in some stretches westward. When I would get on the sections of interstate late at night I would "Let the Big Dog Eat" and would stretch the Cobra Jet out pretty fast. Just as I would get to enjoy the new interstate it would switch back over to US 80 so I would have to slow down. About 5 o'clock in the morning, I was going through Jackson, Mississippi and begin to get a little sleepy. I caught myself dozing and decided I better do something about it. I stopped to fill up with gasoline and took one of my little diet pills so I could stay awake. When I was in college, I could take one of those little pills and be good for another 16 hours of being wide-awake. Shortly, I was wide awake and soon found that the interstate bottlenecked at the Mississippi River because the bridge construction was so time consumptive.

Shortly after crossing the Mississippi, I got back up on I 20 and actually made it to Arcadia, Louisiana, which is where she lived, in record time. By the way, Arcadia is where Bonnie and Clyde met their end. I spent the weekend in and around Arcadia and even made a trip into Texas, with her dad and stepmother. Although it was good to see my girlfriend, the highlight of the trip was that someone in Arcadia owned a 1968 ½ 428 Cobra Jet Cougar. I spotted it on the side of the street and stopped to look it over. I never did find the owner and thought it was neat to run into another very limited production vehicle that far away from home.

Wade Claxton's Z 28 Camero

After my visit was over, I bid my girlfriend farewell and headed back home. I had made note of all of the stretches of interstate where I planned to air out the little "Jet" on the return trip. Throughout Louisiana I did just that. When I arrived at Vicksburg where we had to get off I 20 and get on US 80, to cross the Mississippi River I ran into a traffic jam. The bridge that crossed the Mississippi River at Vicksburg was so narrow, a steel super-structured bridge, that if a wide load planned to cross it, traffic had to be stopped on both sides until it could get by. As I sat there waiting for the wide load to cross, I heard an engine rev up behind me and I looked in my rear-view mirror to find a Z 28 Camaro in behind me. He would rev his engine up, and I would rev mine up in answer. We did this several times waiting for that wide load to pass. After the traffic cleared, we were in a bit of a traffic jam until we were able to get back on Interstate 20. As I pulled out on the interstate, I accelerated fairly rapidly. He pulled over into the left lane, in an attempt to pass me, which was not going to happen. Every time he would try to go by me, I would accelerate just enough to keep him behind me. We did that for several miles on I 20, and I was running speeds in excess of 130 miles an hour to keep him from passing me. I played with him for several miles when all of a sudden, the hair on the back of my neck bristled up as we were going up a hill. Don't ask me what it is, but sometimes I could sense a situation, like I did then, and avoid trouble. I let off the accelerator and got on the brakes and of course he zoomed by. I was running the speed limit when I topped the hill and spotted the Mississippi State Trooper with his radar gun pointing to the crest of the hill. At the bottom of the hill were two more state troopers and two more at the top of the next, I found my competition in the Z 28, pulled over by yet another trooper. I waved as I passed and deep down inside knew that I could've easily been pulled over too. Also, I knew that if both of us had topped the hill at the kind of speed we were going, side-by-side, they most likely would have wanted to charge us with racing, which likely was more expensive than speeding in the state of Mississippi. I don't know what happened to my friend in the Z 28, but I bet he had some choice words for me.

On another occasion, Billy and I had gone to LaGrange, Georgia to see his old girlfriend. She had arraigned a blind date for me so I made the long trip with him. On the trip there, we noticed a very sharp S-curve on the highway, between Eastman and Hawkinsville. I told Billy to make note of it, so that we could try the C J 's road race suspension out on the return trip.

We took our dates to the West Point VFW for a dance. That was when one of their friends at the table pointed out a fellow, it turned out he was my date's husband, across the room looking strangely toward our table. The friend said that I did not have to worry about him, it was her boyfriend over by the bar that I needed to worry about. I didn't even know she was married, and here I was at the "West Point Knife and Gun Club" with my .38 Special pistol locked up out in the Mustang. There were also two folks there who quite possibly had no love loss for me, and also might desire to do me bodily harm. It wasn't long after that that I persuaded Billy and his date that it was time to leave. I did not want to have to fight my way out of that bar in a foreign land. I was very relieved when we loaded up in the Cobra Jet, and I cranked it up. I placed the pistol under my right leg and was happy we were headed back toward Lagrange.

We had an enjoyable weekend and on the return trip, we recognized the landmarks and set up for the S curve. I went into the first part of the curve at somewhere around 115 mph. I kept slightly accelerating through the first half and then into the second half of the curve. As we came to the exit of the S-curve, I glanced at my speedometer which was a good ways beyond 120. The tires had balled a little but had never lost traction. I was even impressed with how well that road race suspension took those curves, designed for 50 miles an hour. The last trip I made through there I discovered that the DOT had redesigned the S curve and softened the curvature greatly.

Wink, Billy and I had been messing around at Billy's house and were coming into town on County Farm Road. I was running somewhere over 100 miles an hour, and we crossed the creek approaching Philippi Church. Some guy in a yellow Chevelle had been following me fairly closely. I had decided long before passing Crosby Chapel Road that I was going to see just how close he could stay to me. As I entered the curve there, I was doing something in excess of 110 and he was trying to follow me. I accelerated going into the curve, and the fool tried to stay with me. I had no trouble taking the curve. As a matter of fact, it was a curve to the right, and I did not even veer out of the right lane. As we looked behind us, the driver of the yellow Chevelle had not realized what kind of curve we were going into. Instead of trying to hold it under power he made the mistake of hitting the brakes in the middle of the curve. The centrifugal force pulled him to the outside, and he almost went through Mr. Beckworth's cornfield on the left. The yellow car was swishing back and forth as he was trying to get it under control and keep it out of the ditch. I bet he had to go change his britches after it was all over.

I had practiced taking curves, so that if I did have to run from the law, I would be proficient at taking those curves at higher speeds, to avoid capture. That car would take a curve almost as good as a friend of mine's little MG would. I tried to follow him one time in Jacksonville Beach with my white Mustang and he made me look like a monkey. Every time I started to gain on him, he turned again, and I'd have to get on the binders to keep from going where I did not want to go. Jerry could drive that MG pretty well. Although my Mustang had much more horsepower my suspension could not stand up to that of the MG. He is the reason I wanted a road race suspension under my Cobra Jet. It worked really well, and I delighted in taking tight curves and cornering with that Mustang.

Winkie and I played in a rock band on the weekends. It was a way to really enjoy making music but also to have a little extra spending money when you needed it. We had played in Waycross one Saturday night, and he decided to go to the all-night café and have oyster stew which was a treat we often enjoyed. Afterwards we started home about 2 o'clock in the morning. As I made the turn onto Georgia 15 in Blackshear, I eased down on the throttle and was doing probably about 100 miles an hour as I exited the city limits. There was a garage and wrecker service on the left. As I passed it caught a glimpse of something out of place, in the corner of my eye. It looked like a police cruiser backed in amongst the wreckers. I told Winkie to turn around and see if anything pulled out of that parking area. He told me that he thought he saw something pulling out, but it didn't have its lights on. I told him to keep watching and eased on up to about 125 mph. Wink informed me that the headlights had come on and so had the "Bubblegum Machine" on top. I took my speed on up and momentarily hit the intersection at Bristol. I was glad it was early in the morning, and there wasn't any traffic, because of how fast I went through that intersection. After passing Bristol, I ran it on up to somewhere in the 140 mile per hour range. I had to calculate the speed by the RPM's because my speedometer only registered 120 mph. As we approach the county line, we hit the drainage of the Big Satilla Creek. It was a pretty long expanse where you could see over 2 miles behind you. As I topped the hill into my own county, I had Winkie watching for signs of my pursuer. As we went into Appling County, he informed me that he could not see anything in the rear. Not being satisfied with that as I approached the intersection of Georgia 121 which turned toward Surrency, I backed off the speed enough so that I could accelerate into the curve that was part of the intersection. As we went into the curve, my back tires tried to break loose, but my road race suspension held like it was supposed to.

Winkie let out in a strange voice "You got him outrun! You can slow down now! You don't have to kill us!"

That is the only time I ever saw my buddy, Wink, show fear, in a fast car.

Not wanting to take a chance of being apprehended, I made my way back to where Wink's car was parked, via several remote country roads. I then only crossed the main roads twice in route to my house. I never liked to take a chance, and when the "Rabbit Got in my Blood" I avoided main roads, and I always parked the car behind the house to avoid detection. I had learned long before not to run in a straight line because of that General Electric overdrive the police had in their cars.

On another occasion I was headed to Alma to chase girls. I was running in excess of 130 miles an hour, when I spotted cause for alarm in front. The Georgia State Troopers used VASCAR in order to determine your speed. They would set out two bleach jugs 132 feet apart and time you as you went through that measured course. They could quickly determine your speed using this method. I saw them in my front and the two jugs with the State Trooper cruiser backed off on the edge of the right of way. I immediately got on my disk brakes, for all I was worth and managed to slow down to the point that I pulled in beside them in their parked cruiser. I never made it through their marked off area but as I pulled alongside their car, I reached in my wallet and took out my driver's license and handed it to the trooper that was next to me. They were amazed. They knew I was speeding but had no proof because I never crossed through their little clocking area. They looked at me for a moment and then handed my license back to me said.

"Boy! You need to slow that thing down!"

"Yes sir!" I replied and headed on into Alma.

Racing Local Favorites

Freddie Stone's 1966 Chevelle

One of the three times that my Cobra Jet lost a drag race was against my good friend Freddie in his 1966 yellow Chevelle. He had just gotten the engine blueprinted and we went out to race on a surface treatment Highway in the County Farm community. I did not get off as well as I should have but recovered and was closing the gap in a hurry. Unfortunately, my friend Billy and I had measured the quarter-mile in that location with a steel tape. We had painted straps across the highway for the perfect quarter-mile. As we drew close to that quarter-mile stripe I was gaining rapidly on Freddie but he crossed the stripe a couple of feet in front of me although I blew by him immediately, I could not argue that he did not beat me in the quarter-mile. Funny thing was he was racing another friend Richie and his Chevelle and something happened to Freddie's engine causing Richie to win the race. Richie later ran Jody in his 440 cubic inch Mopar with Jody coming out on top.

440 Cubic Inch Mopar GTX

This caused Jody to believe that he could outrun me badly. We met up on a really good asphaltic concrete road to settle the score and I must've beat him eight or nine car links in the quarter. This was due to the fact that I got off better than I did against Freddie, which made all the difference in the world. Later on, Jody came to me and said that although I ran him in the quarter-mile but he could outrun me on top he and because he could run 160 miles an hour. I told him that if he could run 160 that he could surely outrun me on top end. We went out to the 10 mile straightaway between Surrency in Baxley on US 341 and I told him to get everything he had that I would be behind him and when he had it all to turn on his left blinker if I was still there. That he did. I had quite a bit of accelerator pedal left although in the flying mile Billy and I had clocked my Mustang at 152.5 mph. I blew by Jody so fast that it was almost like a normal pass on Highway. I never heard anything else from him after that I guess maybe I had proven just how fast the Jet was.

There was a fellow in town that operated the Texico filling station in the middle of town. He owned a Camaro that was touted to be fast. He even had a local sign painter paint its name on the side, "The Prospector". Several of the local boys had come to me saying that he had challenged me to race. I sent word back saying that I would be in Claxton on Sunday at the drag strip and if he wanted to come and grudge race me it would be fine with me. We headed out that Sunday to the drag strip only to find that it was closed that day for some reason, so our grudge race did not materialize.

Later that week the challenge from the "Texaco Terror" (as we called him) came again. I agreed to go race on a county road where Billy and I had measured out a quarter mile. Although I preferred to race without much of an audience, it was hard to meet those challenges without half the town being there too. I always figured the "Funeral Procession" leaving town would attract the wrong type of attention (the Law). When we left town, the entourage headed out that way behind us. The area we had marked off was about 8 miles out. We lined them up and when the signal was given to start, he actually jumped me, due to the fact that he had slicks and I had street tires. Nevertheless, my "Pony's Killer Second Gear" reeled him in and passed him before I shifted to third. I beat him handily and was pulling away. Third gear in that Mustang was awesome and I would wind it to 6800 R P M before shifting to fourth, which was usually about when I was crossing the finish line. It only had a 3.50 to 1 rear gear ratio (Ford's factory drag racing Cobra Jets had a 4.30 to 1 ratio to maximize the quarter mile performance). Upon returning to town his entourage came back to me, with all kinds of lame excuses as to why I beat him. The real reason was that his car was just not fast enough for the Gold Mustang.

There were lots of fast cars in our area. It did not take long for the Cobra Jet to prove its speed in the quarter mile and on top end. One by one I accepted challenges, won the races and picked them all off.

I was racing a 426 cubic inch Street Hemi RT Dodge one night, and the owner of it said that since he had an automatic transmission there was no way he would run me from the dead start. He wanted to run from a 5 mile an hour roll. This suited me, because when I was not utilizing slicks on the Cobra Jet, I would have difficulty with my starts especially on surface treatment roads, like I was running that Dodge on. I accepted his proposal, and we got side-by-side at 5 miles an hour. The passenger in his car, whose window was rolled down, yelled "Start", and we took off. I pulled that hemi in first gear, then I pulled him a little more in second and had him by several car links when I shifted from 3rd to 4th gear. I knew that the little Cobra Jet was torquey but had no idea that he could pull the Street Hemi in every gear when pulling and torque on the upper end was the forte of the 426 Mopar Hemi.

I raced a fast 396 cubic inch Chevelle with 375 horsepower from Jesup one night. Although he was renowned in the neighboring county for being the fastest Chevrolet there. My Cobra Jet was more than enough for the job. I beat him seven or eight car links at the end of the quarter. I had known him for a good while before the race and he told me afterwards that he had heard that my Mustang was fast but had no idea it was THAT fast.

I raced several 440 cubic inch Mopar's, including two 440 Six Packs which were equipped with 3 two-barrel carburetor setups. I handled each of them quite easily. Although one of my three defeats had come at the hands of a good friend from Bacon County, and a 440 cubic inch, four barrel RT Dodge. Although I

71

had him off the line, when I tried to power shift, my clutch never left the floorboard, and I had to immediately back off. We later raced him again and I quite handily defeated him. He told me he was sure that I would have won that first race without mechanical difficulties.

There was another fellow in town named Jody who had a 440 cubic inch equipped Chrysler Corporation car. He challenged me to a drag race but when the car pulled up alongside mine, he was not driving but one of my buddies that I graduated with was. It was strange that most of the time I would only race one of two drivers, Boozy and Freddie, regardless of the car and it was Boozy this time. My philosophy was to beat you just as badly as I possibly could, so that I would not have to worry about you anymore. So, I outran that car some 14 or 15 car links.

I thought that I was through with him until one night at the Tastee Freeze, when he approached me and said, "you can outrun my car in the quarter but there's no way you can outrun it on top end."

I inquired "Just how fast is that Mopar?"

"It will run 150!" He stated

Although my 120 mile per hour speedometer would run out of numbers and third gear. I knew that Billy and I had clocked The Jet in the flying mile and had calculated at just above 152 miles an hour. He and I went out late one night, to a stretch of road between Baxley and Surrency, that was a 10 mile tangent section. I told him that I would get behind him, and for him to get everything that Mopar had. If I was still behind him, he was to turn on his left blinker when he had its top speed. I was just behind him when the left blinker began to flash. I had what felt like an inch of accelerator pedal left. I punched the little "Jet" and passed that

Mopar like you would normally pass a car on the road. I've read somewhere that a normal pass takes 15 mph additional speed beyond what the car is running for you to pass. Enough said!

I raced a red GTO from home, realizing it was no match for the Cobra Jet. I beat him so far it was ridiculous. I later found out from the boy that owned the car that the only reason he challenged me was because he wanted to see my car run up close. He knew he didn't have a chance but wanted that front row seat in a race with the locally "Famous Snake Man."

A fella came from out of town with a fast Camaro. He approached me at the Tastee Freeze about a race. I was never one to back down from a challenge, although his reputation had preceded him. He was known to have a fast car, and I guess he had come into town like the pool shark looking to take down the local champion. As usual, I did not want to draw a lot of attention because it would attract the local Sheriff and Georgia State Troopers. I gave him directions how to head out of town in one direction and turn back so as to meet me at the appointed location without an entourage following. We met at the prearranged quarter mile and we turned them on. He was fast, but I still managed to be about four car links ahead of him when we crossed the quarter mile. We met up later in the Tastee Freeze and discussed the race. All the local race fans were upset that we had snuck off and raced without them knowing and being able to see it. That suited me that we had not attracted attention from the law enforcement community. They watched me close enough as it was. I did not need to do anything else to draw their attention to me any further.

Locally on several occasions I had the opportunity to race against Plymouth Road Runners. Their engines range from 383 cubic inches displacement to 440 cubic inch displacement.

The fastest car I ever raced was a Street Hemi 426 Barracuda. I was not impressed with the way any of the Road Runners performed, although they were lighter than some of the other vehicles, I raced. I could not tell they were significantly faster. The fastest Mopars I ever raced was that Street Hemi Barracuda, but I was still able to pull him several car links. I seemed to put a little more distance between us in each gear and was really walking away from him in third.

I raced several fast Fords, including 427 cubic inch Galaxies, 428 cubic inch Torinos and Cyclones. The closest race any Ford product gave me was probably the GT 500 Shelby Mustang in Daytona. I still beat him about five car links, which was pretty good considering my car was then pure stock and ran much better after I put in the dual point ignition, got rid of the smog crap and tinkered with the vacuum linkage. This was the only work I ever had to do on it but the addition of 8-inch wrinkle wall slicks which made a tremendous difference. Instead of having to come off the line at 1800 RPM and slip the clutch, I could pop the clutch at 4500 RPM with the slicks on it. I never saw it but one of my friends, Bruce, said that when I did in fact come off the line at 4500 with the slicks on the car, that my front end would lift, and my tires would "Jump a Milkshake Cup" to quote him.

I raced all the fast cars in my county and all the surrounding counties that were street worthy. Those that weren't, I would race at the drag strip. My car only suffered the three heads up defeats during that time.

At the Savannah Dragway, Hubert Platt and Randy Prior of the Ford Cobra Jet Factory Team were there. We had a good long conversation, and Hubert gave me a sheet with everything to do to my Mustang to bring it up to what had been done to the factory Mustangs. The cost of the parts was about $1000 with most of it being the cost of a 4.30 to 1 Traction Lock rear end, complete ham.

My friend Billy, although he was a Chevrolet man, worked on my Mustang. When people ask us which was fastest, his Camaro or my Mustang, we would tell them we were on the same team but did not race each other. This would frustrate them greatly. Billy finally started telling them whichever car I was driving would probably win the race, which let me know his confidence in my driving ability.

Once when I was at Mr. Pete's Station talking to Bruce, a fellow pulled up in a Mustang. He came over to where Bruce and I were talking and informed me that I needed to get Tiger Paw tires like his. He kept on telling me how much better they were than my Goodyear Polyglass. I told him I was satisfied with my tires. He kept on aggravating me and keeping Bruce and I from discussing what we had been discussing. After a while, I had enjoyed just about as much of him as I could stand, when he insisted, I should

75

try his tires on my rear. I agreed and we jacked up both rear ends. We put his Tiger paws on my rear. He was still bragging about how well his Tiger Falls would hold, and like I said before "I Had a Level Bait of Him". The traffic was light and when I pulled out on US 1, I dumped the clutch at about 3000 revolutions per minute. Blue smoke board from under my rear end, leaving two black streaks. The streaks only got blacker when I power shifted the gears. I left two black streaks almost all the way to the Tastee Freeze. It looked like the Mosquito Sprayer had come by. When I returned to the station, rubber was flaking off the Tiger paws. I had broken the rubber in the tires, and they were no longer good for anything but starting a fire. I reinstalled my Polyglass, telling him that Tiger Paws did not impress me worth a Damn.

It finally became difficult to get a race anywhere around home, which slowed my street racing down considerably. I had always wanted to go back to Gainesville and try my Cobra Jet on that track. I still wish we had taken it instead of Neil's car that weekend. No telling what I could have done there in my second national event.

Fast Chevrolets

Souped Up 327 Cubic Inch 1956 Chevy

My friend, Billy, had a 1956 Chevrolet two-door, in which he had installed a 327 cubic inch and had begun to do things to it to make it go faster. It had a special cam in it. Knowing now what I didn't know then, it probably was producing way more than 350 horsepower, maybe close to 400. That Chevrolet would fly. I remember on one occasion when I returned from the drag strip and had been impressed by a dragster with a flip top front end. I told Billy about how impressed I was with it, because you could access everything in there with no difficulty. The engine compartment of my 1966 Mustang was on the smallish side, and some actions were difficult to perform because of that (the problem was later compounded on my 1968 Cobra Jet because the engine compartment was not much bigger and that 428 cubic inch was a hunk). As a matter of fact, the Ford dealership said that the instructions for changing the spark plug called for disconnecting the motor mounts and jacking the motor up. We later resolved that problem by removing the piping for the smog system. There were enough pipes in there to plumb a 2 bathroom house. We also removed the smog pump, which Billy thought might make a good motorcycle supercharger, to let the engine breathe better. But that is another story. Now back to Billy's 1956 Chevy.

He never fully told me what all he had done to it, but a couple weeks after describing the flip top front end that I had seen on a dragster, I was at his house and he said, "come here and let me show you something."

To which he took 2 pins loose and flipped the front end of that 1956 Chevy up just as I had described. He blew my mind with that trick. He also had installed heater hoses running from the grill to the air cleaner and created his own ram air package.

Blue 1962 Chevy II 327 Cubic Inch

I also went with him to Statesboro, where he purchased an old, underpowered blue Chevy II. We towed that crippled thing back to Baxley, and he commenced to remove the running gear from his 1956 Chevy and inserted it into the much lighter Chevy

II. When he finished, we took it for a test drive, and that sucker would fly. It had so much acceleration that it would lay you back in the seat until he let off the accelerator. He would rev near 8000 RPM's with that small block Chevy powerplant. I was with him one day, when he was running through the gears on US 1 South of town and the clutch exploded as he hit second gear. Parts of the clutch came up through the floorboard of the car, and to this day I believe the rubber floor mat lying in the floor saved both of us from shrapnel wounds in our legs. I can still remember how that rubber mat raised up at the sound of the explosion. There were holes in the floorboard and one of the exhaust pipes was cut in two, which could've been our legs. That was an impressive car. Although from the outside it did look like much, just a plain old Chevy II. But it sounded great and ran like the wind.

Me in Billy's 327 SS 350 HP Chevy II

1966 327 Cubic Inch 350 Horsepower Chevy II

He later purchased a 1966 Chevy II SS 350 which housed a 327 cubic inch engine with a Holley four-barrel carburetor sitting on top. That beast produced 350 horsepower, and in that light of a car would fly. I have thought back over the years and tried to decide whether his first Chevy II with his old hopped up 327 cubic inch or the SS 350 was faster. It is hard for me, in my mind, to compare the difference in the two because they both were superfast. As a side note I was riding with him in that red SS 350 one day. We were beginning to head home and started out of town. He had just "burned rubber" on Main Street. This was something we all liked to do. We were heading out Bay Street toward the country where he lived. Suddenly the chief of police was in behind us with his red lights flashing (they were red back then not blue).

Billy looked at me and said, "Do you want me to outrun him?"

To which I replied, "Why not?"

Billy got down on that little red rascal, and pretty soon we were beyond the city limits and the chief of police was nowhere in sight behind us. A friend of mine who lived on Bay Street said he was sitting on the porch when all of that occurred. He said the tires barked on that red Chevy II and it jumped, accelerating faster than he had ever seen anything. He said that presently the chief of police came by with his dodge spitting and coughing unable to run. Now this boy's father was a deputy sheriff, so he paid particular attention to this occurrence.

That Chevy II is still around the County and I see it every once in a while, which brings back memories of the "Good Old Days".

1969 SS 396 Cubic Inch Camero

Billy later acquired a 396 cubic inch Camaro. This thing was pretty doggone fast in its own right. But it wasn't fast enough to suit him. He came by the house one day and asked if I still had my "speculating money" (this was money that I kept stuck back in case I ran across something that I wanted to buy, knowing that cash would get the better price.) I told him that I did, and he asked if he could borrow some of it for a few days, to which I readily agreed. What were friends for but to help one another out in times of need? I didn't ask what he was going to use it for, but he told me he was going to use it to purchase an engine he had found. I later found out it was the L 88 racing version of Chevrolet's 427 that he intended to install in his Camaro because the 396 cubic inches engine was not a hot enough engine to suit him. For a long time, I was one of two people in town that knew about the acquisition of that engine. That car was fast, really fast with that 427 cubic inch engine in it. I could not drive it well because I was used to a Ford clutch which let out about three quarters of an inch from the top, whereas the Chevrolet clutches had to hit the floorboard in order to shift. Subsequently, I was never good at power shifting a Chevrolet. People would ask us, which was faster, mine or his. To which we would reply that we were on the same racing team and did not race each other. This was not a lie, for I never felt the desire to race Billy. I would tell people that he would outrun me, and he would tell them that mine would outrun him, so that would leave them in total confusion. Judging from the elapsed times, they were pretty close to each other in performance. He had always said my driving would be the difference and I don't know if that's true or not, but it was very flattering coming from a person whose opinion I valued greatly.

On one occasion Billy was challenged by a fellow from Alma who owned a 428 Cobra Jet, Mach 1 Mustang. We had run our cars against the clock and our measured quarter mile enough to know how fast his Camaro was. We knew my elapsed time in the quarter mile, and we knew what most Mach 1 Cobra Jets would run in the quarter. We both figured he had that race handily. At the Tastee Freeze before the race, he had been asked to open his hood so that the folks could see what he had under it. This he did without hesitation because you could not look at that engine and know it was any more than a 396 cubic inch Chevrolet. They went out to race and Billy beat the Mach I, but not nearly as much as we all thought he might. Upon returning home he opened the hood and found that one of the spark plug wires was pulled off the plug. The thought crossed my mind that he might have done that himself to keep the race close, to then run the boy for money later. He told me who he suspected of doing that little "deed", but neither of us had spotted him doing it.

There were lots of folks around who would've liked to have witnessed Billy and I running our two cars against each other, which never happened. If it had, we would not have allowed anyone to be a spectator because it would've been only for our satisfaction as to how our cars drove.

When he bought the SS 350, he sold his old Chevy II to Wink, who was younger and was also a good driver. Wink was a little wilder than either Billy or me. He liked speed, and I'll tell you another story about him a little later.

One day Winkie and his friend Tommy were riding out by the high school. He saw some girls out in front of the school, and decided he would impress them. He shut down on that Chevy II, and from the reports that I had of the incident, the tires were burning so badly that it looked like the mosquito sprayer that came through the town in the evening putting out a smoke (probably containing in DDT). He not only got the attention of the girls, but he also got the attention of a Georgia State Trooper who took off in hot pursuit.

Realizing this, Winkie got down on that little Chevy II and did like we all used to do, headed for the country. That little Chevy II had a 4.11 to 1 rear end and would accelerate superfast, but it was not very good for top end speed. He turned on a county dirt road and headed out toward the county line with the Georgia State Trooper following him in hot pursuit. A friend of mine, Boozy, said that his family was setting out tobacco plants in the field on his daddy's farm, when the Chevy II came flying by. He told me that it came by so fast that it flipped all the tobacco plants upside down and they had to replant them.

Wink was burning that state trooper on the dirt road, and he fully intended to totally lose him and hide when Tommy, his passenger, convinced him to slow down and surrender. The state trooper had hit a wash out on the dirt road and had torn up his front end on the cruiser. As he approached the Chevy II, with his .357 magnum revolver drawn, Winkie decided (too late) that stopping might have been a mistake. Winkie was handcuffed, and they were both put in the rear of the trooper car and taken to the Sheriff's office. The trooper was so shaken up from that pursuit, that he was still shaking when he got there. Wink had to call our friend, Marvin, and get bail posted, so that he and Tommy could be released. He later told me he wished he'd never slowed down.

SS 396 Chevelle

Compliments of Shawn Tootle

He later had a Chevelle that was plenty fast. Fast enough to cause his competition at the Vidalia drag strip to pull a pistol on him to intimidate him before the race began. It was obvious that the other fellow figured that Winkie could take him, and he was supposed to be "King" of that class. Winkie was upset, stemming from that altercation, and probably had not forgotten it to his dying day. He also carried a pistol from then on. I see that fellow from time to time and remember what he did to my friend on that particular day. I am still angered by it.

Both Billy and Winkie were my very closest friends, and both were good behind the wheel of an automobile. I never really felt the urge to race against them, because we were all on the same team, as far as I was concerned. Although we were steeped in competitive juices, that did not extend toward each other. We were satisfied in helping each other do the best they could do.

Wink and I played in the same rock band and were around each other almost all the time. He had acquired a fast motorcycle and at our band's practice session one night, he decided to see just how fast it would go down the street that our practice house was on. Weyman, our drummer, was sitting in his GTO Judge in front of the practice house when Wink took off down the street. Suddenly we saw the headlights of that motorcycle shining in the treetops and shining all over the place. Winkie had lost it and had a severe crash. Weyman took off in the Judge to check on him. Seeing he was injured, and it appeared to be severely, Weyman scooped him up and took him to the hospital emergency room. I quickly closed up the practice house and jumped in my Mustang. I burned the road up between the practice house and the hospital. When I got in the hospital, I heard Winkie in the emergency room hollering. That was a great big orderly standing there in the hall. I asked him how my buddy was doing and he quickly told me that he couldn't tell me anything. As I said he was a big man, but I grabbed him by the shirt and ran him up the wall, shaking him and said, "I want to know how he is. Now!!"

Trembling he said, "he be all right, he be all right" and I let him slide back down and put his feet on the floor.

That escapade ended Wink's motorcycle riding days, and he never wanted to get on another one again. I am sure that remembering the fear and pain he had that night was the cause of that reaction.

_____

One night I was riding around and cruising the town. I ran up on Billy and this new girl he had met. They were on his Harley Davidson Sportster. He could not have much in the way of conversation with her on the motorcycle. We agreed to swap vehicles and rendezvous at the Tastee Freeze later that night. I cruised town like "Bronson" on the TV series.

When the time of the rendezvous approached, I started to make my way back to our prearranged location, I was sidetracked by stopping to have a conversation with another friend. We had agreed that if we weren't there at the assigned time we would meet at Billy's house. Knowing I was late arriving I noticed Mustang taillights going down the street that went to County Farm Road which we had to take to go to his home. Upon circling the "Freeze" I did not see my car there and assumed that he had headed home and that it was my Mustangs taillights I saw. I put the 900 cc Harley through its paces, to catch up with him. I loved motorcycles and used to ride regularly with Billy. I was not unfamiliar with the sportster and had no qualms in airing it out. He lived about ten miles out, eight of which were paved. I pushed the Sportster up to over 120 miles per hour but did not spot the Mustang in my front. I maintained a good speed until I came to the hairpin curve in the dirt county road near his house. When I backed way off the throttle for that last turn, I heard the distinct moan of a Holley carburetor in my rear. It was Billy, in my Mustang. He had spotted me leaving town and had pursued me to his house. He inquired as to how fast I was going to which I replied that I was too occupied looking at the road to notice.

Drag Racing On The Streets

The sheriff once described us as not "Bad Boys", he said we were just "Mischievous as Hell". I remember, on more than one occasion, many trips to the "Barrel" to turn them on. Lamar loved drag racing as much as anybody did but was frustrated after my fastback Mustang outran his 289 Cubic inch Mercury Comet after he had souped it up. He was not happy with the fact that my car was faster than his, so he made one last move in the Muscle car realm.

Lamar later purchased a 442 Oldsmobile that was a fast vehicle also. I'm sure that part of his impetus was because my white Mustang would outrun his red Mercury. The 442 had a Rochester carburetor on it. The Rochester would give a distinct sound. Kind of a whine, as it sucked air into the carburetor to mix with the gasoline. Holly carburetors had a distinct moan when they were doing the same and Carter AFB carburetors had an even different sound. You could tell by the sound what kind of carburetor was on the engine. I can remember riding with Lamar when he would "Shut Down on It" in his 442 and that Rochester would begin to whine. I swear it appeared as if the gas gauge was faster than the speedometer because when that Rochester started sucking fuel and air into it, it didn't take long before Lamar had to stop and buy gas.

The original Oldsmobile 442 got its name because it was a four-barrel, four-speed with dual exhaust. The engine displacement was not 389 cubic inch but a 400 cubic inch and produced quite a bit of horsepower. It was a decent running muscle car and Lamar's car was equipped with an automatic transmission, which eliminated the necessity to make good shifts. I don't know what the elapsed time was for his car and I'm not sure if he ever ran it on the track and clocked it.

Afterwards when I purchased my Cobra Jet Lamar lost all interest in running fast and took him a new bride. He then concentrated on playing softball and umpiring and refereeing sports games.

There is no doubt that the group of guys that I grew up with, had we all been born 100 years earlier, would have had fast horses. It must have been in our DNA because we all like to go fast. Lamar actually had two of the fastest horses in town, and my friend Joby had one of the three fastest horses in the county. I rode all three of them growing up and thoroughly enjoyed the feeling of the wind in my face as they stretched out at a full gallop. When I was young, I liked to ride my bicycle fast. I even took the fenders and the tank off to make it lighter, so it would go faster. As I got older, Joby had horses, and we like to ride them fast. In the seventh grade I would rush to the house after school, put up my books and jump on my bicycle. I would ride cross country to Joby's house and would beat the bus on which he and his siblings rode. Before we could ride horses, we had to feed the hogs. We quickly dispatched that task and rode horses until near dark, when I returned home. This would be a daily event because I loved to ride. I loved the wind blowing in my hair and face. That was the most speed I could experience at the time.

Lots of boys from my hometown would go to the drag strip on Sunday and race. There were also some accomplished racers from home who raced in the higher classes. I remember many local heroes driving Fords, Chevrolets and Mopars that raced at the local

89

and regional tracks. Some of them raced with pretty good results. I remember one GTO named the Cobbtown Special. I remember many that had no name written on the side and no sponsorship. They just raced for the love of racing. I often thought that a dragstrip around home would be nice. We actually had a dirt track oval at Dunn's Lake. It was 30 miles to the nearest drag strip, and I believe it would have been successful. Most of the better drag strips were where they utilized some of the additional runways of old military airports that dotted the South Georgia landscape. Mostly they had concrete paving, were wide and were really lots of fun to race on.

We had one local drag race hero named Jerry. He raced on all of the tracks around Georgia and in the south. He was a superb driver and could really jam gears. I remember once when he was racing a Prefect (English Ford) station wagon at Vidalia. When he made his last shift, the clutch blew up and some of the shrapnel hit some of the spectators on the sideline. I'm sure that the Prefect had a Mopar engine, because he was racing with the local Mopar dealer out of Glenville, Georgia at the time. He later raced Mopars with full-blown Hemi engines inside.

Not too many years ago, my son and I went to a drag strip in Douglas and Jerry was still racing and was still good at it. He had been injured in a race car and walked with the use of crutches but still can cut a light and drive hard.

There were two cars from neighboring Jesup, "the Chinese Bandit" (a 426 hemi equipped Dodge) and the "Wooly Booger" (a 427 Ford Galaxy). Both were extremely fast and absolutely thrilling to watch. A friend that I worked with purchased the "Wooly Booger" and later raced it out of Glenville, Georgia.

There was at one time, a 1967 Ford Fairlane Tunnel Port 427 that was around Toombs County and Appling County. I knew all the folks who owned that thing. Although it was not a street legal machine, it was a bear on the drag strip. It came equipped with a 427 cubic inch side oiler engine with a large "Tunnel Port" intake and two Holly four-barrel carburetors sitting atop. The fuel system sat up so high that the Fairlane was equipped with a blister hood to allow room for those two Holly four-barrels. That car was one of Ford's R code offerings as was my Cobra Jet Mustang. I never had the opportunity to run my Cobra Jet against it, but with my slicks on I could have most likely given it a fair run. It probably still would have cut me, but I do believe the little "Jet" would've made a good showing based on my elapsed times versus the elapsed times of the tunnel port both of which were around 11 seconds.

My friend Bruce, the one that had the Henry J, at one time, owned the Wooly Booger, the Tunnel Port Fairlane and a fast Mustang to boot. He was a pretty good driver himself and a really good friend. He was also a pretty good mechanic.

There were folks from the surrounding area some coming from as far as Savannah and even Andersonville, South Carolina to race in Vidalia. There was even a jet car there one time which was awesome to see. Gene Cromer from Andersonville, South Carolina was a known drag racer that visited our area. Gene Cromer had also brought a 1940 Willis Coupe named "Moonlighter". I can remember the first "Funny Car" that I ever saw was brought to Vidalia. It was a 1964 Falcon, with a 427 cubic inch engine in it. The engine was fed by a Hilborn injection system. Now later, funny cars became a class of drag racing a funny car was an exhibition car. Although Gene's 40 Willis Coupe would do wheel stands that were controlled by wheelie bars on the rear. It made a beautiful arcing wheel stand, as he came off the line. When the little blue Falcon pulled up to make a solo run, he pulled such a wheel stand that sparks were flying from the Falcon's back bumper, as it drug on the pavement. The only other vehicles that we had ever seen do those kinds of wheel stands were Dodge and Ford specially designed pickups with the engines in the rear. Those things were awesome to see and inspiring to hear. Later there appeared a red Ford Tunnel Port Fairlane and campaigned it around in South Carolina and Georgia.

Willys Coupe Gasser

Some of the dealerships around South Georgia also sponsored cars, most of which were in the normal classes. I attempted to convince the local Ford dealership to sponsor my Cobra Jet but was unable to secure any assistance, although their sales benefited from my car's performance.

Wheel Standing 1964 Falcon

The biggest draw though was the local folks both racing in class and "grudge racing". That was when you could run your buddies without fear of the local police capturing you for street racing. It was, by far, the best place to see where your car stacked up against the local competition. We had some great times there and settled many a dispute about whose car was fastest. Since the racing at the drag strip was at best once a week, we had to settle some disputes on the local back roads. Unfortunately, the Sheriff and his deputies, along with the Georgia State Patrol, were always trying to catch us. Sometimes they succeeded. Other times we were able to outrun or evade them to avoid being captured. I always considered that discretion was the better part of valor. If I could run and hide and avoid capture. I was better off and certainly was money ahead.

I hope the statute of limitations has run out because I surely don't want the local sheriff knocking on my door and carting me off to jail for my past sins and iniquities after reading my writings.

Once I was lined up at the "Barrell" to race a Chevelle, when the deputy pulled up behind in his new gold Torino Cobra. I immediately took flight. I was amazed at how far I was ahead of him when I started my "Evasive Maneuvering" to get him "Off My Tail". It did not take long to lose him. I again went home and parked behind the house.

Escape In Florida

Once when Billy and I were headed to Flagler County, Florida we were cruising along in my Cobra Jet on I-95, South of Jacksonville. I was in the left lane, running about 90 to 95 miles an hour. I was not encountering any problem with the traffic as they all stayed in the right lane and let me pass. I have always had this "Sixth Sense" that has kept me out of lots of trouble through those years of driving fast. I noticed way back behind us, in the rearview mirror, a car that would quickly pass one or two cars and get back in the right lane.

As I looked back there, I told Billy, "I think we have inherited a tail"!

He turned in his seat and after a while agreed with my observation and evaluation. I knew that we weren't but just a few miles from St. Augustine, so I floored the little Cobra Jet. Quickly my speed went from 90 mph to over 140 mph. I watched the mirror and sure enough he had detected my flight. He pulled out in the left lane and started coming for me with his "Christmas Lights" on. I looked up in front and saw the overpass for one of the interchanges looming ahead. As soon as I cleared the overpass and was far enough down the hill that I knew my taillights would be shielded from my pursuer, I hit those disc brakes and popped into a slot between two cars matching their speed.

I watched the mirror to see the Florida State Trooper come over the top of the overpass at a high rate of speed. Just as he passed me, I saw the red glow of his brake lights momentarily and then he kicked it in the behind. I don't know if he thought he recognized me, or if he was at a loss as to where I could have gone.

Nevertheless, Billy and I decided it was a good time to pull off at the next interchange, go to Howard Johnson's and have supper. We figured by the time we ate he would either have forgotten us or would be in Miami still looking for those Mustang taillights. The disc brakes were almost as important as the speed that night.

Another funny thing happened on that trip. We were on the way to Daytona Beach to watch the Paul Revere 250 on the night of the 3rd of July and stayed in the infield at the Speedway all night for the Firecracker 400 the next day. We picked up my cousin Henry in Bunnell and headed to the track. When we came out of the tunnel into the infield were told that the Mustangs were all parking at a place along the fence between turn four and the tri-oval. Since we like to be agreeable guys, in an act of solidarity, we turned left instead of going to my normal place which was between the number one and two turns. We set up there for the night as we were parked parallel to the fence. We attached a chenille bedspread to the car and to the fence like a lean to tenant and settled in for the night.

Mercury Racing Cougar

That night Dan Gurney and Parnelli Jones drove their 1968 Mercury Cougars to victory but to me the star of the show was a Tequila Yellow Mustang driven by a magazine editor that was the fastest car on the track. His trouble was staying off the wall and staying out of the fence. It was a great race for Ford Motor Company that night. Since the race started at midnight didn't end up till about 2 o'clock in the morning, we were sprawled out on our blanket under our makeshift lean to, to try to get what sleep we could, before 11 o'clock the next morning when the Firecracker started. We had bologna and cheese, light bread and mayonnaise in the cooler that was to serve as supper the night before, breakfast the next morning and dinner at noon.

The next morning, when I was aroused from my semi-comatose state, I looked around and Billy was nowhere to be found. Henry was over there to my right just snoring away. Billy was MIA. I crawled out from under the lean to and swept the area looking for my friend. There he was. He had attached himself to two men and their wives who had a camp stove out and were cooking breakfast. I watched as Billy was served up bacon, eggs and toast, which he wolfed down before returning to my Mustang. He did the same thing in Atlanta one morning at the Atlanta International Raceway. He must have had this hungry look about him that made people feel sorry for him and want to feed him breakfast.

Seek and Destroy

I raced the local boys more and also the ones in adjoining counties, with regularity. One such night, driving my Cobra Jet, Billy and I had "cruised" the Debby House drive in restaurant that was located in neighboring Alma. I had a habit of fanning the accelerator at slow speed which made the quad exhaust on that Mustang gurgle.

I was "gurgling" through the parking lot when two boys sitting on the hood of a 1957 Chevrolet said, "We got an Impala that'll turn you on".

I hit the brakes so fast the Mustang stood on his nose and Billy leaned out the window and said, "You smooth talking SOB, you talked us into it."

We went out on the Douglas Highway to a filling station, where there was a small crowd gathered around a black Chevrolet Impala. Since Billy and I were on a "Seek and Destroy" mission, he had my nickel plated .38 special Smith and Wesson in one back pocket and 50 $20 bills in the other.

The guy with the Impala asked, "which one you want to run the Impala or the pickup?"

My reply was the only logical answer to his question, "Which one is fastest?"

1967 427 Cubic Inch Impala

It was decided I would run the Impala. Then he brought up "running for money" and said he would not race for less than $500 a run. This was Billy's cue, and he extracted the wad of $20 s from his back pocket and began to count. The owner of the Impala quickly backed down, as he saw we would not be bluffed. It was decided we would run for fun. We went out to this place where the county road started in Coffee County, ran through Bacon County and ended up in Ware County. I do not believe that the grass had been mowed all year because it was about 4 foot high. As we started to line up the cars, I told him I preferred the right lane if it was okay with him. My reasoning was that sometimes the CJ would jump to the right when I hit second gear, and that road was so narrow that I feared I might jump into the side of his car. (It was only 18 feet wide and felt closer than that because of the uncut grass towering on each side.) It almost looked like a green tunnel. We were given the signal to go, and sure enough when I hit second gear, it jumped slightly to the right and my right rear wheel ran off the pavement and started spinning in the dirt. This allowed him to get a slight lead on me. I quickly recovered and got the CJ under control. Then I began to track him down. When I hit third gear, I blew by that 427 cubic inch Impala. By the time we crossed what they said was the quarter, I had him by 10 or more car lengths. It was an impressive victory, after accidentally spotting him so much. That must have humiliated him to have been beaten that badly, after getting a better start. He later started making excuses and told me the reason that I outran him was that his tachometer was hooked up wrong and it caused the car to run hot, which was a bunch of bull. I just whipped him badly. The only thing "Hot" was my Mustang.

On another occasion I was running a supposed hot Camaro, in our town, that was rigged up for the drag strip. I bested him at least as bad as I did that 427 cubic inch Impala. His excuse was that his motor mount broke, and it caused his distributor to hit the firewall and break. Bull again, he was just whipped! They all had to have an excuse, although the reason was that I was faster.

It really did not take long for my 428 Mustang to eliminate the catcalls and challenges at the Tastee Freeze. Most of the races that I got were just people who wanted to see my car run and knew they had no chance of beating it. I could ride through the Tastee Freeze parking lot and would be deafened by the silence. This was just as I had predicted back in the day.

After my buddy, Freddie, with a 1964 Chevelle had beaten me, he supposedly raced another friend Richie who had a 396 cubic inch Chevelle (375 HP, I think) later that night. Supposedly Richie had beaten him. Then Jody, who had a 440 Dodge RT had somehow beaten Richie. Now you must understand I had already beaten Jody's car severely.

I didn't really beat Jody, just his car, because most of the time if I raced another car, I was facing one of two drivers who were both excellent drivers, Freddie who owned the fast 1964 Chevelle and Boozy who owned another 396 cubic inch Chevelle. They were like hired guns that folks with supposedly fast cars wanted every advantage possible. They would get them to drive their car in their stead. Both were good friends, and I never minded it, but it was humorous that folks with quasi fast cars had no faith in their own driving abilities.

Years ago, when I didn't have anything fast, I loved to go and watch the street races. Although none of the cars then were fast, compared to what we had later, there was still fun to watch. We went to the barrel one night riding with one of the competitors. We were standing in the edge of the woods preparing to watch the race when the Sheriff's cruiser topped the hill. The competitors scattered. Since we were afoot, we headed into the woods. Instead of chasing the drag racers the Sheriff's car pulled off where we were. I later found out that the GBI agent (who was married to my cousin) was with him. When they took off, we headed for the dense woods. I ran until I found a clump of gall berries that I could hide in and dove into the middle of them. I saw the flashlights as the beams raked around in the woods. I lay there trying to control my breathing, so that they could not hear me, since I was almost out of breath from running. They stomped around in the woods for a good long time and then returned to their vehicles. The GBI agent got awfully close to me, at one point in time. I tried to mold myself into the dirt and must have been successful, for I was not discovered.

Once they departed from the scene, we gathered together to talk about our situation. One of my friends, Jimmy, said that he was in the middle of a clump of palmettos and that the Sheriff had stepped on his hand. He said that he bit his tongue so as to not holler out and was sure glad when the sheriff moved on and took the weight off his fingers. That night Jimmy, Roy and I walked nearly 5 miles back to town, because the drag racers did not consider us important enough to retrieve. They were too busy "Getting The Heck Out Of Dodge." That was the first time that I had to walk back to town, but not the last.

Over the years I quickly learned to have my car there so that I could drive back to town. That was the last time I went to watch a race with no mechanical means of escape and return. I learned that it was best to take your own car with you so if you have to make an escape your destiny would be in your own hands and not in that of someone who might run off and leave you. We would all get rabbit in our blood when the "Man" would appear on the scene.

On another occasion at the "barrel", we were lining up to run when the deputy quickly came up behind us in his brand-new Cobra Jet Torino. This fast pursuit car was purchased just for the purpose of being able to run us racers down. I looked up and seeing him and his flashing lights in my rear-view mirror I took off with all I had and headed South on Georgia 15 highway. He decided to chase me down, which was a mistake for two reasons.

Number one my car was faster and number two I had a road race suspension under me and was not about to run "straight line" away from him. That was not my style. I would make as many a turn as possible to avoid being captured by the authorities. Thank God the statute of limitations has run out. I quickly put a tremendous amount of distance between our vehicles and begin to make turns onto county paved roads. I turned left at the Children's Home then left again on Poor Robin Road and came into Baxley on Holmesville Road. I crossed US 1 and hit Bay Street taking it to Beach Street (where I lived). I quickly crossed US 341 and got to my house. I pulled the car into the rear of the house, as usual, hiding it. I didn't see the deputy after I turned off at the Children's Home, but I didn't take any chances. It didn't pay to. Those boys had what we used to call a "G E overdrive" which was there two-way radio system.

One time a deputy was chasing me. He was the deputy that I really liked but I did want him to catch me. I made several turns and hit a paved road that I knew had a little road on the left that went up behind the tree line that was parallel to the road and to the top of the little hill where the road was cut through. As I approached that location, I knew I had enough lead to do it so I hit the brakes, whipped the Mustang to the left up on the dirt road and behind the trees and sat there watching as he flew by not even noticing that I was up on the hill by him. I had seen that in the cowboy movies and decided it might not be a bad trick to have it in my bag.

That deputy was the only law enforcement officer that could come to the Tastee Freeze at closing time and get all of us teenagers who were parked in the parking lot to leave. When the other law enforcement would come by and say, "Okay boys go home and see mama!" That would only make us want to stay there worse. This deputy would come over there and spot one of us that he knew.

He would give that person the signal to come to the car and would say something like, "Beau, you know these folks get nervous when you boys hang around here after closing. Why don't y'all find another place to bunch up and have your talks and such."

I had a great amount of respect for that man and would most likely have done anything he asked me to since he would ask you to, so respectfully. Mr. Johnny was the epitome of a law enforcement officer.

There was a time when I was cruising around in Alma, looking for girls and/or drag races, I made the mistake of burning rubber to close to where the deputy, Speedy, was. He let out after me, and I put it in the wind. Speedy was the only one who had ever caught me and caused me to pay the only two fines I ever paid in front of Judge Wheeler in Bacon, County. I made the trip to Baxley in 11 minutes covering those 20 miles in near record time. Then I performed my evasive maneuvers by hitting all the back streets and again went to the house, hiding my car.

There was the time when I had blown the clutch out from under the Mustang and was waiting for the parts to arrive (since it was an 11 ½ inch Holloman Moody diaphragm clutch, not something that was in every parts room). The Ford dealer had given me a 1965 Galaxy as a loner until my car was ready to go. Billy and I had gone to Hazlehurst chasing girls and were backed into a parking place at one of the local haunts. That Galaxy was such a dog. It would hardly run, with that 352 cubic inch family car engine in it. Also, when you would get to 50 miles an hour the headliner would break loose flipping the springs and it would come down around your eyes. The exhaust system was worn out. We were sitting there watching the traffic and had just shut the engine off (which had a broken manifold and sounded a little loud), when the occupants of a black barracuda to my left leaned out the window and asked me.

"Is that Ford bad as it sounds?" They asked.

"Naw man!" I responded, "it only sounds bad."

"I didn't think it was. I ain't never seen a bad Ford" he retorted.

"Well, this one ain't bad." I replied "but I got one at home that might fall in that category. I'll come up here next week and show you just how bad it is."

"You just do that." He said with a smart mouth. "You wanna' fight".

Billy, who is a pretty good size fellow, sat up to his full height in the seat and said, "we can do that too if you want to!"

The guy in the other car decided he didn't really want to. They even ask us to go with them to the bar which was down the street and have a beer.

The next weekend I brought my Cobra Jet back to Hazlehurst and when approached about racing me, the guy with the black 340 Barracuda told me he no longer wanted to race. I would have loved to have shown him what the taillights of that Cobra Jet looked like, if he would've obliged.

I also later learned that the fellow in the car with him that night had a reputation for fighting and winning. I don't know what saved Billy and I from having to fall out and fight with him other than just blind luck.

Another time I was at the Tastee Freeze in Hazlehurst talking to a good friend of mine. We were drinking a suds and he flipped his beer can down just missing my barefoot.

I had nicknamed him "Punk" and said to him, "Punk it's a good thing that can didn't hit my foot or I might have had to whoop you"!

That same guy with a reputation of fighting was standing there. He said to me "I wish I had a can"!

When he said that I handed him my near empty beer can and stuck my foot out, like an idiot. He looked at my foot and flipped the can off into the bushes. I guess I had bluffed him twice. I am glad I didn't try a third time because you know they say, "the Third Time Is the Charm".

1969 429 Cubic Inch Torino Convertible

At this point I am compelled to tell a side story. Every vehicle that I have owned, I had paid for. On the other hand, my sister, Liz, upon graduation from high school and beginning at the University of Georgia was presented a 1969 Ford Torino convertible with a 429 cubic inch engine as a graduation present from high school. I almost croaked. That thing was pretty, cool and fast as all get out. I have always ragged her about that, how she was the "Chosen One". I even bought my mother's Pontiac Bonneville when she bought a new car (that was one of only two non-Fords I ever owned.) That was what I was driving when I got T-boned in a wreck and suffered a pretty severe neck injury. My son Billy was a baby and was with me and his mother in the car when it happened. I didn't go to the doctor to start with because I didn't think there was anything wrong with me. The next morning, I went to a dove shoot and on the first shot I dropped my shotgun to the ground in severe pain in my neck and arm.

Everyone Had a Fast Car

There was a point in time, around town, when everybody had a "muscle car". We had fast Mustangs, Torinos, Cyclones, Fairlanes, Galaxies and Cougars. The Fords had 289 cubic inch high-performance, 390 cubic inch high-performance, 406 cubic inch police interceptors, 427 cubic inch side oilers, 428 cubic inch Cobra Jets and 429 cubic inch engines. We had Impalas, Chevelles, Camaros, Corvettes and other sundry Chevrolets. The Chevrolets came with 327 cubic inch, 396 cubic inch (with all different amounts of horsepower) and 427 engines with lots of horsepower. The Mopar boys had Darts, Roadrunners, RTs and Superbees. They came equipped with 383 cubic inch, 426 cubic inch wedges, 426 cubic inch Street Hami's and 440 cubic inch six packs. We also had many an Oldsmobile 442 and Pontiac GTOs along with every other muscle car you can name. If we had all those vehicles now in pristine condition, we could be multimillionaires. Those old muscle cars have been selling on Barrett Jackson for unreal prices.

Weyman, who was a drummer in our Rock Band, had a pretty GTO Judge.

1969 GTO Judge

Weyman Allen

The Mopar boys all stuck together as would the Bowtie guys. I was a Blue Oval type of fellow. Although we were not as numerous as the Bowtie and Mopar we had some fast cars in our stable also. I cannot begin to tell you how many 396 cubic inch Chevelles there were around town. And there were so many Mopars, especially Roadrunners that I bought a tag for the front of my Mustang that said "Beep, Beep Hell".

1968 Barracuda

1968 Dodge Charger

Bowers Collection

1968 Plymouth Roadrunner

I can remember being parked at the drive-in movie theatre and hearing a car crank up. I would be able to identify it by its sound. The Mopar starters always made an extremely loud whine. You could tell the difference between Holley, Carter or Rochester carburetors as they accelerated. Those sounds are all burned in my mind since they were a distinct part of my youth. Although all the four barrel and three deuce carburetors sounded good on high-performance machines, I am partial to the moan of a big Holley. I love to hear that sound to this day.

1986 F-150 Four Wheel Drive

The last vehicle I had with a big Holley was a 1986 Ford pickup equipped with a 351 cubic inch HO engine. Although the Holley was not as big as the one on my Cobra Jet, it still had that distinct Holley moan as you pressed the accelerator to the floorboard. I took it to a friend, David, who helped me take off all the plumbing from the smog system and discard the smog pump. We plugged the holes with short bolts, and this made a tremendous difference in the performance of that pickup.

All of those muscle cars sounded good, and all performed pretty well, although some were more powerful than others, it was a time that I believe never will be equaled in Americana. Things are not now where a young man can do what we did. There is too much traffic, there are too many deer, houses, and too many police to even think of being a "Wild Child" as we were in those raucous 1960's.

You could ride through the Tastee Freeze parking lot in Baxley, and all the guys would be backed into the parking places with the noses of their cars pointing toward the driveway. It seemed to be commonplace back then, but the whole parking lot would be full of muscle cars. Although the number of car owners who actively participated in drag racing was not nearly as large as the number that owned automobiles capable of it. Some lacked the courage or confidence to go wheel to wheel with someone else, and others feared tearing up their cars. But I can envision the scene as we rode through that parking lot. If we had our cutouts disconnected, we would push in the clutch and blip the throttle as we tried to show out. Some would get "Squirrely" enough pop the clutch, and "Squeal the Wheels" slightly. Others would just ride up and down the strip showing off their cars, hoping someone would notice.

I tried to be a man of action so I was just crazy enough to race anytime someone would suggest it. I loved the thrill of being side-by-side in the exhilaration of the acceleration of the automobile. I never liked losing, but sometimes it was inevitable. I have always been a very competitive person, and I guess that translated into my car ownership and therefore into street racing and strip racing.

One friend of mine, Billy, who was a little bit older, had the most beautiful burnt amber 1966 Fairlane 500. It was probably the prettiest car of that model that I ever saw, and it ran too. He would take it to the drag race and would win regularly. The car came with the 390 cubic inch four-barrel engine but I am absolutely not sure that was what was in it for most of its life. I have always suspected that he swapped out a 427 cubic inch in its place which would explain why it was so doggone fast. Several years later, I spotted one that looked like it pulled up in the woods by a house in Telfair County. I pondered purchasing a car, and restoring it, but never got around to it.

1966 Tunnel Port 427 Fairlane

Bruce, after having his Henry J, had a pretty fast dark blue 1965 or 1966 Mustang. He liked drag racing and did it with regularity. He would race at the drop of a hat. He was a pretty decent mechanic and could make almost any car faster than it would've been. At one time he owned that special Ford Torino with a 427 cubic inch Tunnel Port engine and the 1963 Ford "Woolie Booger" with a hot 427 cubic inch in it.

Another person in Baxley who owned that 427 cubic inch Tunnel Port Ford was the bass player and leader of a soul band. His name was Tyrone, but everybody called him Big T. He always liked fast cars, and once he wanted to race me in my Cobra Jet Mustang. He was driving a 396 cubic inch Chevelle at the time. He asked me what I had under the hood, and I told him a six cylinder. We went out and ran the quarter mile and I smoked him severely. That 396 cubic inch Chevrolet was no match for my Cobra Jet. When he and I met up a little later, he wanted to see my engine, so

I lifted the hood. He saw that big FE Block engine sitting there and the ram air package on top and knew he had been had.

"I thought you said that was a six cylinder?" He asked.

"I did but I forgot about the extra two helpers it had" I replied.

To this day one of the boys that was in the car with him, which has been a friend of mine for years, will not let me forget that incident. He has to talk about my "extra two helpers" under my hood.

1969 Chevelle SS 396

Complements of Wade Claxton

The car that you saw the most in our area was the Chevelle. At one time I thought that everybody and his brother had one. It was like every second car you saw was the Chevelle. The Chevrolet dealer and the Mopar dealer in town sold many more fast cars than the Ford dealership did. The 396 cubic inch engine came in horsepower ranges from 325, 350, 360 and 375. It seemed as though there were hundreds of them in the county, which I believe contributed to the local Chevrolet dealer being so affluent. After 1965 just about every one of them had a 396 cubic inch engine. Some from out of town even had 427 cubic inch engines in them. I remember racing one of the 427 cubic inch Impala from Rochelle, Georgia with my Cobra Jet. He ran a good race but still fell to the side when the quarter mile was complete. I had known him when we were in college, and we were pretty good friends so it didn't bother him very much that I outran him.

1969 Cobra Jet Cyclone

One of my close friends, Lewis, was injured in an accident at work and was paralyzed from the waist down. He still loved speed and ended up with a 1969 Cobra Jet Cyclone. Although it was equipped with hand controls to facilitate him driving, it was faster than most cars around. He did not let his handicap stop him from enjoying life, even though it presented some obstacles. He would drag race at the drop of a hat and frequently won.

One memory of him that sticks out is, that when we would be low on money and want to go to the drive-in movie, he would get in the trunk of my 1966 fastback Mustang, and after I had paid and gone in, instead of having to stop to let the passenger out the trunk, and risk being spotted by the management, he would crawl through the door into the back of my Mustang which would have the back seat folded down and by the time I came to a stop he would be in the front seat beside me. We were never captured although several of our friends who had to stop behind the projector building and let their passengers out had been captured. He could slide through that opening exceptionally smooth and slick. He started his drag racing before his injury in a 1954 Chevrolet straight six cylinder. I remember the night when he and another 1954 Chevy were racing and after the race while turning around, they collided, not more than one half mile from the G B I agent's house.

1969 Mach I Cobra Jet Mustang

Bowers Collection

Two brothers, who were close cousins of mine, came to me one day saying that they wanted to order a new Cobra Jet Mustang. They were looking at a 1969 Mach 1 body style. They asked me to help them with the order so that they would get all the goodies that I had in mine. I went through the order form and filled out the order with all the high-performance package, road race suspension and ram air package. They ordered it and when it came, a beautiful red Mach 1, they were excited. Instead of a four-speed it was equipped with an automatic, but that sucker could run pretty well. I never had an opportunity to run against it with mine, because there again we were not just cousins, but close friends also. They were active in racing it for a little while.

During that time, I filled out quite a few orders for vehicles making sure to include the high-performance equipment. I guess I was somewhat of a celebrity at the time and did in fact know the ins and outs of everything that Ford offered. The Ford dealer was supposed to give me a small finder's fee when I prepared an order but never followed through with it.

I constantly read and studied to find out what they were doing and really desired a Ford Single Overhead Cam 427 cubic inch engine because from what I read it was a fast engine and produced upwards around 500 horsepower without even being tinkered with. It was Ford's "Hemi". Later, after I had quit racing Ford, who was getting on away from racing at that point in time, was selling the SOHC for $3995. I really would've liked to have owned one of them, although it would probably not have made a very good street engine. I was thinking how nicely it would run in something like my old 1960 Falcon.

Ford's Hot Engines

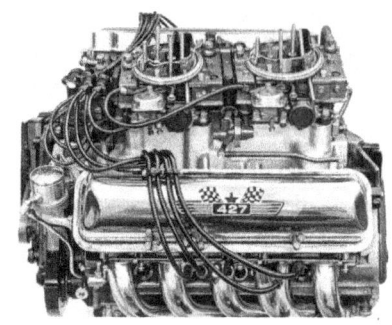

427 Ford Wedge

428 Cobra Jet Engine

Ford SOHC Racing Engine

Some folks have restored old muscle cars in their possession to this day. They love them and the era that they represented.

At today's market prices for late 1960's muscle cars the boys in my town owned cars that would total into the millions of dollars. I found the body of a 1968 Cobra Jet (R code VIN) Coupe Mustang on eBay a while back. This was just the body with no motor, transmission or rear end. They were asking $36,000 for the body only. My Cobra Jet cost $4000 in 1968. If I had all those cars in an old tobacco warehouse, I could be a wealthy man at the Barrett Jackson auctions. One just like my Sunlit Gold Cobra Jet sold the other day at auction for $209,000. To be such a small town there was almost every variation of muscle cars there. One of my good friends had a GTO Judge that would fly. Several had fast Chevelles and Camaros. I had some good friends driving the Mopar's. Although we were all highly competitive and drove different brands and preferred different brands, we were part of a fraternity of sorts. If someone had built a dragstrip in town and opened it up on the weekend, we would have been very happy. They could charge a fee and allow people to grudge race and most likely would've made pretty good money. Without a doubt that would have kept lots of folks from racing on the street. Our only options were to go to a dragstrip at least 30 miles away or to street race.

Other Fast And Cool Cars

One day as I was cruising the strip, I spotted an odd-looking vehicle. From the front it looked like a 1966 Mustang, but from the rear, it looked like a Falcon Ranchero. I got my Mustang into action and finally got him to pull over at a place called the Weatherly Barn South of Baxley. I got out and talked with him for a while and looked over his piece of work. He was in the auto body repair business and had married the front end of a 1966 Mustang to the backend of a 1966 Falcon Ranchero. It was equipped with a 289 cubic inch high performance with a close ratio four-speed and had a 4.11 limited slip differential. The interior and instrument cluster were all Mustang. It was a unique car, and I really appreciated what he had done to it. I told him as he left to get down on it and let me hear that high-performance scream. He obliged by leaving two long black streaks of rubber, and quite a bit of smoke as he made his way on toward Florida.

1966 Mustang Ranchero

I once spotted a 1967 Cobra making its way through my town. I got behind him with my 289 cubic inch fastback 1966 Mustang at the Dairy Queen and stayed close on his rear end as he made his way through town. When he turned left on Georgia Highway 15, I guess he had had enough of me pestering him, so he got down on it. The Cobra, which had to have been a 427 cubic inch, squatted and took off so fast that he was quickly out of sight. I would've liked to have tried him on a heads up although I don't think I would've stood much of a chance, judging from his acceleration. I would try anybody, regardless of how big their engine was and how fast the car was, with that little Mustang. There was one assurance in it, if my Mustang had slicks, I would most likely beat them out of the hole. Although that little 289 cubic inch was not any match for the big engines that were around when running the quarter of a mile, I could get out of the hole with any of them due to my quick reaction time.

Early Falcon Dragster

A fella came through one day with a 1960 Falcon on a trailer behind his pickup truck. He pulled off to get gasoline and I spotted the Hilborn injectors sticking out through the hood. I stopped to visit with him and learn a little about his car because it had a for sale sign on the window. It was a G Gasser and looked pretty neat with the big slicks and traction bars on the back end. It was a bored and stroked 302 cubic inch engine, sitting in the compartment, under those injectors. He informed me it was for sale for $1100 (which was way beyond my budget at that time), and that he turned in the high 12 second elapsed time with it. I was excited and wished I had the money to buy that beast from him. I had no idea that within a year, I would on that Cobra Jet Mustang which would far exceed in the quarter mile elapsed time that Falcon Gasser could do.

1963 Falcon Sprint 260 Cu in. HP

Not too many years ago I was working in a rural area about 50 miles from home. I was on one of the back roads when I spotted a Falcon Sprint. I pulled up in the yard and noticed the engine emblem on the side. It was a 260 cubic inch high-performance, a very rare engine, and it was just sitting out beside a barn rusting away. That would've been a great restoration. Those early Falcons were light enough that it didn't take much horsepower to make them go pretty fast. In the Cobra the Ford 260 cubic inch high-performance engine was the first engine to generate a horsepower per cubic inch using a carburetor. Chevrolet had done that with the Corvette, but they were fuel injected.

In the 1960's Bill Cosby, who was known for his love of fast cars, got with Caroll Shelby who produced a two of a kind Cobra. One he gave to Cosby, and one that he kept for himself. It had the hot 427 cubic inch cross bolted side-oiler power plant with two Holley 4-barrel carburetors coupled with two Paxton Superchargers producing over 800 horsepower. Cosby admitted in his album 200 miles an hour, that it scared him to death and he gave it back to Caroll Shelby. He made the statement in his comedy album "200 miles per hour" that "I hadn't even cranked it up and it was killing people".

427 Cubic Inch King Cobra

Bowers Collection

He said on the album "take this thing and give it to George Wallace".

127

1932 Ford Deuce Coupe Chopper

Bowers Collection

I can remember back in the early 60's when I would go to
Brunswick, Georgia. There was a drive-in restaurant there named
Twin Oaks. They had a bouncer who worked there, whose name
was "Booger". He had a chopped and channeled 1932 Ford Deuce
Coupe. I don't know the displacement of his engine (most likely a
small block Chevy), but I can still see the chrome valve covers and
the headers and lake pipes that came out from under the hood on
each side and extended to the rear under the door opening. The
outlet was just in front of the back tires. It was a beautiful blue, and
I have always had a soft spot in my heart for that thing. You would
see that type of "Hot Rod" in the movies or in magazines, but that
one was close by and was very impressive.

My Favorite Cars of All Time

Ferrari Testarossa

My favorite all time cars list is topped by the Ferrari (all of them but especially the Testa Rosa and the 500 Superfast). Ferrari was born in 1947 (the same year as I was) enough said. It did not take Enzo Ferrari long to rise to the top of European racing. Ferrari's have won almost every kind of European race. They could take 2.5 to 3 liters of displacement (155 to 180 cubic inches) and divide it among 12 cylinders. They then took 6 side throat Weber 2-barrel carburetors to produce near 200 mile per hour speed. One of their secrets is the 12,000 RPM's to make the horsepower and speed to the final drive of the automobile. In Modena, Italy you could hear the engines whine after 12 hours of test runs at high RPM's. Afterward the engines were torn down and checked to ensure the hand-made engine survived the test with flying colors. I never could afford one but always lusted for ownership of the famous "Prancing Stallion" brand.

Ford GT 40

Bowers Collection

Second on my list is the Ford GT 40. These cars were developed in the mid 1960's to answer Ferrari's dominance in European type racing, including endurance races like Sebring, Daytona and Le Mans. At first the mid-engine car was equipped with a 427 cubic inch behemoth. The engine produced over 500 horsepower but added quite a bit of weight which had an effect on the handling. I remember that in the Sebring race Jim Hall's Chevy Chaparral was leading the race with Mario Andretti in second, driving the GT 40. Carroll Shelby had a sign held up as they passed the pits that read "Try Him No. 1". In response Andretti quickly overtook the Chevy, passing it with ease and began to stretch out a good lead. As the cars neared the pits Shelby had another sign held up which read, "No. 1, Slack Off". The engine was replaced with a 302 cubic inch small block with what was called GT 40 heads. With these heads this small block produced just as much horsepower as the big block with much less weight.

Ford tried to buy Ferrari, but Enzo would not sell it. This enraged the Ford management, and the decision was made they would beat Ferrari whatever it took.

Before going to Le Mans, the engineers placed the GT 40 on the dynamometer, hooked to a computer and ran the 24-hour race on the computer, including pit stops and shifts. They went to the race and took 1, 2 and 3 in the overall race. Carroll Shelby was supposed to be the head of Ford's racing program with the GT 40's but one of the Ford execs overrode him at Lemans. In the last few years, Ford has produced GT 40's that still sport the same body style which is timeless.

I once spotted one in a parking lot in Daytona Beach, Florida and approached it. I looked it over well noting that it was equipped with a 427 cubic inch side oiler. It was awesome!

I later saw one at the Ford dealership in Metter, Georgia. Altogether I've only seen six or eight but loved every one of them.

Shelby Cobra

Bowers Collection

Third on my list is the Shelby Cobra. In the early 1960's Carrol Shelby, a washed-up race driver with a heart condition, found that the AC Bristol (an underpowered 4 cylinder English auto) was no longer going to be produced. He fell in love with the body style and negotiated for the rights to use it. His plan was to outfit the body with a small block U. S. made V-8. He approached Chevrolet and Chrysler Corporation but did not find favor with them. He made his presentation to Ford, and they decided to go into business with him. He had planned on using the 221 cubic inch V-8 that Ford produced. Ford was in the process of changing the displacement of their small block to 260 cubic inches and offered him the use of that engine.

Shelby took the little V-8 and fitted it into the AC body. He attached a Holly 4-barrel carburetor and changed the lift and duration of the cam and produced 260 horsepower which was unheard of in a normally aspirated engine (only the Corvette with

132

fuel injection had done that in the past). When Ford came out with the 289 cubic inch engine, Shelby switched to that engine producing 306 horsepower. Finally in the next years the Cobra was fitted with a 427 cubic inch FE engine (with single 4 barrel and two 4 barrel systems) producing 410 and 425 horsepower, respectively. As a special note, I looked at a 1967 single 4-barrel model in Daytona Beach. The only setback was that the price tag was $7995.00, which I did not have, nor could I afford the payments, if I could have financed it at a bank. I still remember the Wimbledon White roadster in the showroom with the sign "do not touch–may bend". This was due to the super thin metal which brought the weight to 1400 pounds.

Shelby GT 500 KR

Bowers Collection

Number four is the Shelby GT 500 KR (King of the Road) which was the ultimate GT 500. This car was equipped with a 428 Cobra Jet engine. In 1965 Ford let Shelby begin using a fastback mustang with a 289 cubic inch engine. Thus, the GT 350 was born. The louvres in the rear were replaced with little windows and two broad stripes went from front to rear over a hood scoop. When the 428 cubic inch Police Interceptor was installed in it, the car became the GT 500. The GT 500 KR "King of the Road" name came when the 428 Cobra Jet was added. The movies "Gone in 60 Seconds" and "Need For Speed" featured a GT 500.

1968 ½ 428 Cobra Jet Mustang Gold Coupe

Number five is the first that I was able to own. This was the 1968 ½ Cobra Jet Mustang. This mustang had all the running gear of the GT 500 KR, including the road race suspension. Mine was a coupe which was produced in limited numbers (some accounts indicate only 50 were built).

In early 1968 Ford produced a limited number of Mustangs, with the 427 cubic inch single four-barrel engine in it. I had originally wanted one of these, but when they tried to order it at the Ford dealership, they were no longer available.

In mid-1968, as Caroll Shelby was preparing simultaneously with Ford to utilize the newly engineered 428 Cobra Jet engine, Ford began producing the Cobra Jet Mustangs and Cougars. According to records Ford had to produce 300 of those Mustangs in order to make them track legal. That production goal was met with the fastback. The convertibles and coupes were in addition to that number. Having owned one, I fell in love with the car and all its performance capabilities. Looking in some of the publications that ranked production cars, the only one that outperformed the fastback Cobra Jet was the 1964 Fairlane

Thunderbolt with the 427 cubic inch and with the lightened front end. The difference in the quarter mile was in the tenths of a second. My coupe was 300 pounds lighter than the fastback which produced a slightly better horsepower to weight ratio. In the reports in the magazine the elapsed time they recorded for the fastback Cobra Jet was 13.50 seconds. I am sure that was with speed shifting and not power shifting. The first time on the track my coupe Cobra Jet turned in an elapsed time of 12.83 seconds. I was of course power shifting which produces a better ET (elapsed time). If they had tested the coupe instead of the fastback, it may very well have outperformed the Thunderbolt Fairlane.

Roush Mustang

Number six on my list would be the Roush Mustangs of all kinds. There are several different stages of them, all of which perform superbly. These go all the way up to the supercharged models which make great horsepower and performance. In the showroom at Daytona Beach, Florida they had one of each stage.

1964 Fairlane Thunderbolt

Number seven on my list is the 427 cubic inch Thunderbolt Fairlane. It would've been a great vehicle to own, although it was not quite as street worthy as the Cobra Jet Mustang. I have seen the Thunderbolt in action on the drag strip, and it was awesome to watch. When they had been modified and were running in the "Modified Production" class, they ran some right decent times. There was a white Thunderbolt out of Florida that I would see regularly. The Tunnel Port 1967 Fairlane was a version of the Thunderbolt.

1969 Mach I Cobra Jet Mustang

Bowers Collection

Number eight would be the Mach One Mustangs with Cobra Jet and Super Cobra Jet engines in them. I fell in love with a red one that my cousins bought. It was one beautiful machine. Later versions appeared with variations of the 351 cubic inch engine including the Windsor. Some of my friends had them and they would turn it on pretty well. All of these would've been desirable cars for me as a Ford fan

Dodge Viper

Bowers Collection

In 1992 Lee Iococa, who was then with Crysler, collaborated with Carroll Shelby In the development of the Dodge Viper. The Viper was a V 10 power plant in a lightweight sports car chassis. This high horsepower vehicle was to compete with other manufacturers quick cars.

Sunbeam Tiger

Number nine on my list is the Sunbeam Tiger. This vehicle was created when they took a Sunbeam Alpine body and installed a 260 cubic inch Ford engine in it like Shelby's Cobra. The series "Get Smart" featured a Sunbeam Tiger. They were later outfitted with 289's and did some road racing in some of the lower classes. I had a friend that had an Alpine that ran fairly well with the little four "Banger" in it. I could just imagine how the peppy little V-8 could push that little lightweight thing down the road.

1963 Corvette Split Window Coupe

Number ten on my list would've been Corvettes of all sizes and descriptions. Although you can tell I am a Ford man, who loves the Blue Oval and would bleed Ford Blue if you cut me, it would be stupid not to appreciate Zara Duntov's contribution to speed during the time of the muscle car era. His work on the Corvette, and his development of the Chevrolet small and large block V-8's cannot be ignored. A friend of mine in college had a 1963 "Vet" split window coupe that I spent lots of time in. I actually double dated in one (in the luggage compartment). It was equipped with a fuel injected 327 cubic inch engine. It was right quick in its own right. Another close friend, Robert, had a beautiful one that I had the chance to ride in on a regular basis. I do have several friends who have owned Corvettes, through the years, and they are without exception a high-end ride. Duntov's traditions are still carried on to this day, the modern stingrays being outstanding performance vehicles.

Other Chevrolets like my friend Billy's Camaro and SS 350 Chevy II would definitely be included on my list

Mopar Hemi

Number eleven on my list would be Chrysler's Hemi powered cars. Although I always pulled against them, I was quick to recognize how much power they produced, and how they changed the complexion of engine building with the hemispherical heads. The Hemi's were dominant on the drag strip in gassers and funny cars.

1963 Falcon Sprint 260 Cu in. HP

There are lots of other cars like Falcon Sprints, with small V-8's along with Fairlanes, Cyclones and Torinos. Of course, the rest of the Ford stable. Most of the Fords were available with the large block FE engines. Camaros, Chevelle, Barracudas, RT's and Darts along with GTO's and 442's add to the mystique of the muscle car era. There were even El Caminos and Rancheros equipped with large high horsepower engines running the streets back in those days.

Wayne Foskey's 1964 Falcon 289 high-performance

In 1964 Ford installed the 289 high-performance V-8 into the Falcon Sprint which made it an awesome small block car because the lightweight to add to the performance

My two best friends, Billy and Winky, were both Chevrolet men and we got along nicely. Although we had our different preferences in cars, we respected the capabilities of the other brands. I believe that Zara Duntov, who is known as the father of the Corvette, developed most of Chevrolet's high performance engines. Caroll Shelby should rank near the top of the heap when Ford muscle cars are in the conversation.

At this point in time, I have not even taken into consideration the custom jobs that ran the streets too. I had two friends with Ramblers, which were souped up and ran like a house afire. Folks who could not afford the new muscle cars could take older, vintage cars with V-8's and by boring and stroking them and altering the fuel system, i.e. carburetion or adding a supercharger would be able to make a pretty fast car. Some folks who were very talented mechanically could do like Billy did with his 1956 Chevy and make it fast as all get out.

1932 Ford Roadster Hot Rod

Bowers Collection

I did not possess much talent in the physical mechanics of building a fast car. The two talents I had were to research and envision what I wanted to do and drive. Driving was my first love, and going fast was what I wanted to do. Those of us who were fortunate enough to come along during the "Muscle Car Era" got to participate in a time in automotive history like no other. We knew what power and speed was and most of us possessed it.

About the Author

    William A. Bowers, Jr. was born August 5, 1947 in St. Augustine, Florida to William Alfred Bowers Sr. and Lora Elizabeth Tuten. When he was young, his family returned to Baxley, Appling County, Georgia, where he lived, was raised and educated. He is a 1965 graduate of Appling County High School, an Eagle Scout and is retired from the Georgia Department of Transportation as an Area Engineer in South Georgia. Worked as a Consultant Engineer with EMC Engineering for ten years after retiring from the DOT. He is married to Anna Deloris Willis of Toombs County. He is a member of the First Church in Baxley, Georgia.

    William has given speeches and performed living histories at State and National Parks, Historical Societies and other organizations for several years in Georgia, Florida and South Carolina

    He resides still in Appling County and has served as a Boy Scout leader for over 30 years, a charter member and officer in the Appling Grays Camp #918 Sons of Confederate Veterans, was an elected member of the Appling County Board of Education, a member of the Baxley First Church Administrative Board and the Appling County Heritage Center Board of Directors.

He has published three Confederate regimental histories with *the History of the 47th Georgia Volunteer Infantry* being published in May 2013 and *the History of the 27th Georgia Volunteer Infantry* being published in February 2014. In 2016 he published *the History of the 54th Georgia Volunteer Infantry*. This completed the trilogy of Confederate Regimental Histories which encompasses the four companies of Confederate Infantry which originated in Appling County, Georgia. In 2017 he published the *Bowers Genealogy, the Descendants of Benjamin Bowers, Sr., of Pitt County, North Carolina*. His novel *Two Rebels from the Altamaha* and his outdoor adventure book *Memoirs of an Altamaha River Outdoorsman and Other Drivel.*

This Book, *Young Men and Fast Machines* is about the young men from South Georgia who owned, drove and raced Muscle Cars in the 60's.

Copies of all the other books by this author are available at www.bbowers.net

148

www.ingramcontent.com/pod-product-compliance
Lightning Source LLC
Chambersburg PA
CBHW060430130626
46555CB00005B/2290